# PRAISE FOR LON AND *MODERN MERLIN*

"Embrace your magical self as a reality in your life! *Modern Merlin* brings to life the understanding of the unseen world of mathematics and sacred geometry as it pertains to the deeper workings of our *human-ness*. Lon, with eloquence and clarity, has brought to light the essence of a transformative journey into healing and wellness."

—Dr. Barrie Sands, DVM, CVA, HMCT,
veterinarian, scientist, speaker, author, and founder of Illumina Sciencia

"As a master facilitator and adept artist, Lon has an exceptional, elegant, and yet practical methodology for integrating one's purpose into the expression of the mystical transformative realm. What you will encounter and what will become your subsequent journey can only be described as magical."

—Dr. Patricia Murray Suzuki, QME,
CEO, founder of Distinctive Medical Solutions

"Lon, yet again, illuminates us with her wisdom and understanding of the seen and unseen world. Throughout her life, she has guided so many of us through layers of personal elevation and has witnessed the magic that unfolds. *Modern Merlin* is an extension of that and provides a bridge from the old way of thinking to new perspectives and opportunities that reside within."

—Nada Nabulsi, RN, BSN, PCCN

"As a thirty-year student of conscious creation, I found it easy to recognize Lon as a true teacher whose wisdom can guide us in navigating the accelerating energy of our times. Lon offers an intelligent and enticing invitation to awaken to the magic of intentionally co-creating and manifesting our visions, our dreams, and the joyful experiences we desire. I love this book, enjoy!"

—Deborah Smith, serial entrepreneur,
founder and CEO of Rewardify, Inc.

"Get ready for a great adventure! Join Lon as she takes you on a magical spiritual journey to the depths of your soul and the heights of your possibilities. Your life will be richer and fuller, and blessings will abound. Thank you, Lon, for showing us the way to love and holiness."

—Rabbi Wayne Dosick, PhD, author of *Radical Loving*
and *The Real Name of God*

"There is no better authority on the subject of materializing dreams into reality than Lon. She's turned the magic of manifesting into a playbook that's simple, clear, and easy to embody. This book is a must-read."

—Alexander Ryker, Next-Gen Leaders, business growth coach

"This is not only a book about making magic, but also a magical book, which has the power to transform our world. It takes a true master to be able to explain how magic works, and Lon is that master magician. Hold her hand—she will take you into that multidimensional realm where everything is absolutely possible!"

—Ellen Kaufman Dosick, LCSW, channel and author of
the *Cosmic Times—Spiritual News You Can Use*

"Lon is the definition of a Modern Merlin with her Soul Portraits, her oracle decks, and now this book! Dive into this step-by-step guide for discovering your own magic, moving past the ego stories that are holding you back, and becoming one with the Universe."

—Emily Haas, online business coach for coaches

"*Modern Merlin* offers amazing insights and powerful tools for anyone that is into self-development and empowerment."

—Jenna Phillips Ballard, cofounder of Ascension Leadership Academy

"*Modern Merlin* will take you on a magnificent journey into the world of ancient wisdom, contemporary magic, multidimensionality, and manifestation. Lon's impeccable translation of the language of the Universe will deeply impact you and provide you with the insights and tools to support your life."

—Torey Wolford, transformational coach at Ascension Leadership Academy

"Amazing! Lon's transcendence has crossed the boundaries between science and spirituality for the third time. First when she created my Soul Portrait, again with her oracle decks, and now with *Modern Merlin*, where magic and the mind meet. This work bridges the conscious and unconscious mind in a profound way that will manifest into your life."

—Susan Welch, senior engineer, owner of SOUL2SPIRIT,
and creator of Dream Alchemy

"Lon's book, *Modern Merlin*, and course provide us with the necessary tools to live the life we all desire. Thank you, Lon, for developing the steps to make magic real for everyone."

—Seymour Koblin, HHP, founder, director, instructor, and practitioner
at the International School of Healing Arts and author of *Shaping Our Destiny*

"In an ever more rapidly imploding 3D world, Lon's work reminds us of who we really are—divine beings. *Modern Merlin* gives us tools to go ever deeper, to remember who we are, and to access those resources within to be our most authentic selves in these all too interesting times."

—Erika Paleck, director, West Oregon Electric Cooperative

"You may already know Lon for her sacred geometry activations and oracle decks, but now there is another way to play with the magic of multidimensionality. *Modern Merlin* will help you step even further into your own power, shift limiting beliefs, and reclaim your divine right as a sovereign being. Let the magical games begin!"

—Siobhan Wilcox, bestselling author of *Thrive Now Blueprint*
and founder of Sacred Wisdom Academy

# MODERN MERLIN

## UNCOVER YOUR MAGICAL POWERS

BEYOND WORDS
Portland, Oregon

**BEYOND** WORDS

1750 S.W. Skyline Blvd., Suite 20
Portland, OR 97221-2543
503-531-8700 / 503-531-8773 fax
www.beyondword.com

First Beyond Words trade paperback edition December 2021

**BEYOND WORDS** PUBLISHING and colophon are registered trademarks of Beyond
Words Publishing. Beyond Words is an imprint of Simon & Schuster, Inc.

For more information about special discounts for bulk purchases, please contact
Beyond Words Special Sales at 503-531-8700 or specialsales@beyondword.com.

Managing editor: Lindsay S. Easterbrooks-Brown
Editor: Diane Young
Copyeditor: Ashley Van Winkle
Proofreader: Olivia Rollins
Design: Sara E. Blum
Composition: William H. Brunson Typography Services

Manufactured in the United States of America

10 9 8 7 6 5 4 3 2 1

Library of Congress Cataloging-in-Publication Data
Names: LON (Artist), author.
Title: Modern Merlin : uncover your magical powers / LON.
Description: First Beyond Words trade paperback edition. | Portland, Oregon
    : Beyond Words, 2021.
Identifiers: LCCN 2021032933 (print) | LCCN 2021032934 (ebook) | ISBN
    9781582708508 (paperback) | ISBN 9781582708515 (ebook)
Subjects: LCSH: Magic. | Change (Psychology) | Change. | Consciousness.
Classification: LCC BF1621 .L66 2021 (print) | LCC BF1621 (ebook) | DDC
    133.4/3—dc23

LC record available at https://lccn.loc.gov/2021032933
LC ebook record available at https://lccn.loc.gov/2021032934

The corporate mission of Beyond Words Publishing, Inc.: *Inspire to Integrity*

FOR YOU, BEAUTIFUL, BECAUSE YOU CAME FROM
MAGIC AND MAGIC YOU'LL ALWAYS BE.

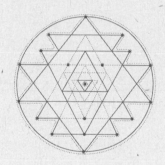

# CONTENTS

# CONTENTS

# FOREWORD

I think many of us have had experiences in our lives that felt like *magic*. Have you ever visualized an empty parking space you need, and "magically" one appears just where you imagined? Perhaps you randomly think of a friend you haven't spoken to for months or even years, and then "magically" they call you out of the blue. Maybe while driving, you get an intuitive hit telling you to slow down, and as you do another car runs a red light directly in front of you. Something inside you "magically" saved you from a collision.

These kinds of incidents happen all the time, everywhere, to all kinds of people. Many of us shrug this off as coincidence or a lucky break. Then there are those—possibly you—who feel something bigger is happening, like a force or energy is influencing the scenario, and this "magical" moment ignites a curiosity to discover what that might be.

If that curiosity has you reading this book right now, you are in the right place, my friend!

*Modern Merlin* will illuminate the phenomena that guide you to co-create the world you want to live in as well as teach you life-long skills and habits through the practical tools it provides. You'll soon be able to harness the power of the Universe and live a joyful, purposeful, and meaningful life.

Personally, working with hundreds of thousands of people through my online company Mind Movies, as well as conducting thousands of interviews with transformational leaders, gurus, authors, and regular people who've had extraordinary life-altering experiences, I've noticed some undeniable recurring themes.

First, in an incredible number of the interviews I conducted, these people described having intuitive abilities or gifts when they were kids. Some could see energy, some could speak to angels or spirits, some could even know or predict things at will. What their stories had in common was that they all suppressed their gifts because the people around them didn't understand what was happening, much the same as Lon (whose personal story you can read in the introduction). Then often, a "magical" incident, like I described above, occurred when they were adults and reawakened their gifts. Now they, like Lon, can no longer ignore them.

Second, I became aware of the growing number of people, from their twenties to their eighties, searching for their life's purpose. They yearn for purpose, knowing that they are destined for more, and are reveling in the pursuit of what that is for them.

And lastly, the undeniable proof of *manifestation*. While teaching people how to get clear about what they want and articulate that through a Mind Movie, visualization, and taking action toward those things, I have witnessed thousands of people manifest all kinds of results, ranging from cars to homes, relationships, perfect health, businesses, even love, just to name a few.

Lon takes you on an exciting journey into magic and manifestation as you uncover the foundational beliefs that shape your world. She uses everyday language to reveal how things work in a paradigm where you are paramount to the creation of your life.

To quote Cypher from the movie *The Matrix*, "buckle your seatbelt, Dorothy, 'cause Kansas is going bye-bye."

Enjoy the ride.

—Natalie Ledwell, author of *Never in Your Wildest Dreams*
and cofounder of Mind Movies

# INTRODUCTION

# MAGIC FOR A NEW ERA

Have you noticed? The world is changing. And fast! Can you keep up? Do you understand what is happening? Do you understand how these changes are impacting your life? And even more importantly, do you have a clue how to navigate all the changes and make your life work?

I wrote this book to support an emerging new paradigm and belief system, to activate the shift in consciousness that is needed to thrive in these new times. When I say "new times," I am referring to the fact that we have arrived at a time in evolution where nothing seems to work the way it did before. Almost all the things we counted on to give us a sense of stability and security no longer provide that. Whether we look at our educational system, healthcare, the political arena, banking and financial systems, or even our spiritual institutions . . . none of them can live up to the role of being the fundamental pillars that our society has leaned on for so long. Even science has evolved to a point where it is introducing an expanded paradigm of how our reality is formed. We, as a collective humanity, are invited to expand our horizons beyond what we know and boldly go where we have not gone before.

It is time we reassess what we believe are the foundations of our reality and the harmony in our lives.

These new times require a
new way of thinking, a new
way of doing things, and a
new way of being.

You and I are going to explore old concepts and redefine them, open ourselves to new concepts and boldly embrace them, and see how all of it fits together. We're going to look at not only what we believe about ourselves and our world, but also how it all works together in a way that allows us to create lives we are excited about.

## What Lies beyond Everyday 3D Reality?

This new time is making us aware of our relationship to energy. Everything is energy, and all energy is connected in a vast and infinite field of unlimited potential that we are part of and in co-creation with—this is the first and perhaps most important fundamental concept to embrace. We are waking up to the awareness that *anything* is possible because our consciousness can operate in multiple dimensions, meaning we can focus on different "layers" of reality.

So far, we have mostly only been aware of the *three*-dimensional layer, where the physical aspects of reality—like our bodies, the stuff around us, nature, our possessions, and so on—have center stage.

When we focus on 3D reality, we depend heavily on linear and logical thinking: we make sense of ourselves and the world, including our relationships with others, by using a form of reason that works with our physical senses. When we think in 3D, we analyze, interpret, judge, and organize information. We also access our interior lives in 3D mode, and when we focus on our emotions, intuitions, insights, thoughts, and memory in that mode, we organize that information in linear ways as well. We tend to judge our thoughts and emotions (and ourselves). We have been comfortable with these material-physical, emotional, and cognitive dimensions of consciousness because that's what brought us here. Yet, these 3D modes of consciousness are so limited for understanding ourselves and the world that many of us have sensed the revolutionary possibility of accessing *other* levels of consciousness.

We are learning how to tune in to multidimensional layers that are of a more subtle nature, like what comes to us through intuition, dreams, emotions, and visions. When we tune in to multidimensionality, we perceive webs of associations and allow patterns of meaning to emerge; we observe meaning as it emerges rather than interpreting or judging.

Our relationship to energy affects more than just our physical, emotional, and cognitive experience and awareness (which help us understand the three-dimensional world of form, matter, and time); it allows us to recognize and affect the multidimensional reality that we live in, whether or not we're aware of our ability to do so.

To navigate among all these levels of awareness is to live in multidimensionality. With practice, we can become as aware of and skillful in working with the energies of multidimensionality as we are in working with the reality of 3D. To stay in harmonious balance with our planet, it is increasingly important that many more of us develop the intuition, insight, and skills that have previously been possessed only by visionaries, intuitives, artists, and shamans.

# Magic Is the New Real

Our growing awareness of energy supercharges our ability to go beyond the 3D plane and access our intuitions in order to participate in the ongoing creation of our experience. We will discover that we even participate in the creation of the Universe itself! Imagination and perception enable us to move between the three-dimensional and multidimensional layers of reality because our consciousness is innately attuned to this energy, since it emerges from the Source that generates all energy.

This new relationship to energy even extends into our spiritual understanding. It can expand our experience of our relationship to the Divine, revealing our own sacredness and fundamental creativity (as in, our ability to create).

Accessing our ability to perceive these subtle layers awakens our potential to work what our ancestors might have called magic and gives us the resources to work miracles. We are no longer exclusively bound by the laws that have governed Earth's three-dimensional world since the beginning of time. We are at the eve of our next (r)evolution-ary leap, as we are awakening to a new reality of a *multi*dimensional world that reflects our thoughts, intents, dreams, and visions.

Did you know that the words we use really matter? As in, they can become matter, become form, become reality. Because words express our beliefs, intentions, feelings, and perception of ourselves and our reality, they carry more than dictionary meaning. They carry energy. We are discovering that our own contribution to the unfolding of

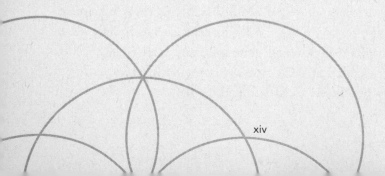

our lives might actually be much greater than we have been told and taught so far. What we think, what we do, what we say—all of it matters. All of it can become real. What manifests in our lives is directly related to our ways of being and doing. How we express our thoughts, feelings, and ideas reflects how we've chosen, consciously or unconsciously, to use our power to create.

Wouldn't it be great if we acted on this understanding that our choices shape our lives? By choosing to be deliberate, thoughtful, creative, and compassionate, we can generate experiences for ourselves and others that have these qualities and that invite others to be creative and compassionate as well. All this is reflected in what and who shows up in our lives. How amazing would your life be if this was your new reality?

## Manifestation is the new word for magic.

Manifestation is the ability to cause and create with intent and conviction, driven by vision and passion, unbound by logic and reason. Imagination is the bridge between the subtle realm of multidimensionality and the 3D world where our visions and dreams are created in tangible form. We are all great magicians with the potential to perform powerful magic in perfect alignment with our wildest imaginations.

We are the Modern Merlins.

# My Story

I grew up in the Netherlands—aka Holland—a small yet progressive and expansive little country, rich in culture yet weighted by history in certain ways. For many—including my parents—war, occupation, evacuations, and death were very real in their lifetimes. Their suffering was reflected in the stories they told and in the silence of their unresolved trauma.

As a highly intuitive child, I felt their pain, their suffering, and their loneliness. I was young and didn't understand why they were hurting or what caused it, but I cried for them. I made their depression and unhappiness my own. Within their paradigm, I was a sensitive—even oversensitive—child. In actuality, I was an intuitive, an empath, able to tune in to and receive information from the subtle layers that were beyond the scope of others. I was already attuned to the (multidimensional) reality that is emerging now: a reality full of messages hidden in the spaces between words, the subtle feelings that arise inside us, and the whispers far beyond the depth of silence.

Of course, I wanted to make things better for my parents. I tried everything in my (childish) power. I loved them as hard as I could, yet it was never enough to take away the nagging sensation of their suffering. I always had a sense that there was more to be done, but there was no way for me to express my insights and no tools to do anything with what I perceived. I had no concepts to describe or explain my experience, no pathway, no road map, no bridge.

I hurt inside, feeling helpless, inadequate, and small. Reality, as I experienced it, was full of clues and indications that came from inside me. I could look at someone and intuitively know where they were hurting; sometimes I sensed it in their physical body, and I could always feel it emotionally. I sensed imbalance wherever it showed up. In people, I sensed the sort of imbalance or misalignment that registers emotionally as sadness, anger, insecurity, dishonesty, confusion, or jealousy. Whatever the disharmony was, I knew what it was right away when I met them. I could pick up on disharmony in places as well: combinations of furniture that weren't working together, layouts that didn't flow, lighting that wasn't suitable, or energy that just felt "off."

No one explained any of this to me. And I didn't have the language to ask if anyone else had this sort of insight or awareness. I didn't know that I was an intuitive, an empath, or psychic. I don't think my parents were familiar with the experience or even with the concepts. So, I was very alone in my world of messages that came from somewhere inside me. When I tried to explain any of it, the response was always that I was "just imagining things" and that it would pass if I waited patiently. It didn't pass. So, I stopped trying to share it with anyone. I kept it all inside, living most of the time in a completely different reality—by myself—than the one I lived in with my family and friends.

My inner world consisted of spaces I could make in my imagination. I created whole universes like that. In the spirit of the series *Doctor Who*—in which the Doctor travels through time in a bright blue,

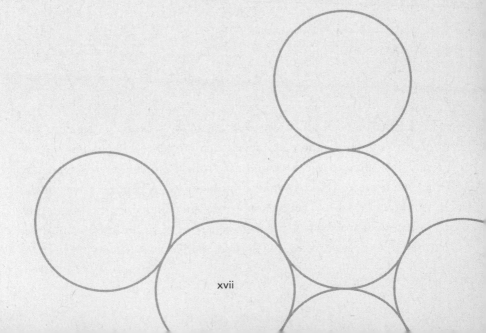

old-fashioned British police box that is bigger on the inside, becoming a place of travel and discovery—I found refuge in my bed. Under my blankets, where I felt safe, powerful, and unlimited, I inhabited larger dimensions of possibility, creation, and magic. Interestingly, my inner universe always utilized the English language, the language that I have come to do my work in now. In my world, magic was normal; the only limitations to what I could create were the boundaries set by my own imagination. And those boundaries were expanded by my intuition, which brought me an awareness of multidimensional reality before I had the language to name what I sensed.

The only limits to what
we can create are the
boundaries set by our own
imagination.

In the outer world I was sick a lot: mysterious, undefined, and unsuccessfully diagnosed illnesses that I often brought upon myself and that allowed me to withdraw from the outside world and stay in my own sacred space under my blankets. Whenever I was in the outer world, I was afraid all the time, surrounded by the mysterious whispers of an unknown that no one seemed to be aware of but me. I felt out of place, weird, lonely, and a failure.

My teenage years were difficult, as I tried to find out who I was and who I wanted to be in life. My experience had already taught me that the options for adulthood on offer were so limiting that they excluded the kind of understanding that was most meaningful to me.

Blessed with beauty and talent in many ways, I was creative, expressive, and artistic. That, in combination with my harmonizing nature, led me to graphic design. I became an independent designer and loved what I did. Translating visions, projects, ideas, and dreams into pictures and images came naturally to me. After all, that is how my inner guidance had always communicated with me: I am a visual intuitive.

It took until my early thirties, when I started traveling outside of Europe, for my world to suddenly open up. I met people in Thailand who talked about ways of perceiving and working with energy and imagination that I had long ago hidden inside me. They spoke in English, and though I had not yet mastered the English vocabulary that would allow me to capture the nuances of my experience and insights, I had never felt so heard, seen, and understood in my life. They used words like "energy," "aura," and "soul" and introduced me to the idea that I was what they called "psychic." All of a sudden *I* made sense; I wasn't odd or out of place. I was an old soul and actually here on earth at this time to support the big shift that was underway. The whispers were about to get louder, and I was here to support the new paradigms as they emerged and to help construct bridges between the realms of Spirit, the multidimensional Universe, and the domain of mundane experience, the 3D world.

I moved to the United States, started a new life in English, and slowly integrated my inner world into an outer one.

Since then, my graphic design has evolved into a body of work that is based on sacred geometry: modern-day mandalas that take us beyond our linear minds so we can be open to the multidimensional language of the Universe. I call these images "activations" because they activate our innate connection to all that is, to the energy that is consciousness, and to our souls. All pieces address large concepts that are the core of the human experience: concepts like magic, love, healing, abundance, connection, intimacy, and multidimensionality. These concepts are fundamental to the way we create our world, our lives, and our relationships with each other. By diving deep into their essence, we can explore our relationship with the qualities they represent and how they are showing up in our lives.

The whispers are here for everyone to pick up; all we need to do is learn how to listen. The Universe is a co-creative place, operating through energy—through magic—to express its unlimited potential. We are all part of it as much as it is a part of us; we are infinitely connected in an eternal dance. Learning how to move with the Universe on the dance floors of energetic layers and dimensions makes us the magicians of our time.

## How to Get the Best out of This Book

This book is set up in three parts, twelve chapters in total.

**Part 1 is all about foundations.** Foundations are important because they form the base on which things are built. We are going to build a foundation for reality by assembling the elements of a new belief system. We are going to pursue new ideas and thoughts that derive from the physical, spiritual, mental, and emotional planes. We are going to develop a new way of looking at things. We are going to shift and expand our perspective on how life works, because it's often not our circumstances that ultimately determine how we feel—it's our state of mind, our perspective. By developing new ways of looking at things—changing our perspective—we can change the way we do things and the way we feel.

▲ Chapter 1: Pathways
To get anywhere, you need to find a path. How do we find our way through this new reality that is emerging, and how do we access the world of multidimensionality?

▲ Chapter 2: Magic
Dive into the world of magic and manifestation and discover that "magic is the new real" and requires belief to manifest.

▲ Chapter 3: Reality
What is reality? How do we know that something is real or not? Explore the difference between three dimensions and multidimensionality and how it is changing the world as we know it.

▲ Chapter 4: Time
Time itself is very much of the 3D world; now that we are moving further into multidimensionality, our relationship with time is changing.

▲ Chapter 5: Energy
Everything is energy. You are, your thoughts are, your words and intentions are. How does this "matter" in who and what shows up in your life?

**Part 2 is about you.** *You* generate your experience of your reality and thus your life. We will explore how what you think, how you feel, and what you say profoundly matters—how it *becomes* matter—in your life. We will look at who you are beyond your physical body and how what you believe about yourself, others, and the world is reflected in the way your life unfolds around you. We will explore your vision and dreams for your life and look at what is in the way of having all that; we will learn how to transcend perceived obstacles and transform challenges into exciting opportunities for growth and change.

▲ Chapter 6: Soul
What is the soul? How do you get in touch with it? Discover how to get in touch with your deep and inner self, the part of you that is infinite and eternal.

▲ Chapter 7: Purpose
What is your vision for your life? What is your "soul purpose"? Your superpower? Why are you here? Discover how your vision can spark your magic.

▲ Chapter 8: The Gap
Are you living your vision? A life that you are genuinely excited about? If not, what's creating the gap, and how can you bridge it?

▲ Chapter 9: Stories
Discover how the stories you tell about yourself draw people and circumstances that align with that story into your life. Write a story that you really love!

**Part 3 is about your life.** Here you are going to put it all together and integrate the new paradigms into a workable model for you. We are going to get really practical and give you tools that you can use daily to navigate the ebbs and flows of your life. We will explore sacred geometry as a powerful tool to help recognize the patterns, repetitions, and cycles.

▲ Chapter 10: Sacred Geometry
"Geometry leads the soul to truth." Plato stated this more than 2,400 years ago! What does it mean? What is sacred

geometry? What does sacred geometry have to do with you?

▲ Chapter 11: Energy Management
How do you manage your energy? How and where do you give it away? How do you refill yourself again? Learn how to manage your energy.

▲ Chapter 12: Tools
Explore various support tools that you can use daily. How are you merging everything together in your life? How do you attend to the blend of your physical, spiritual, mental, and emotional needs from day to day? Download a set of free, powerful templates to work with: https://lon-art.com /modern-merlin-templates/.

Each chapter covers a specific topic. These topics are the building blocks of a new belief system that you and I are going to create together. Each topic is actually a constellation of concepts—concepts within concepts—all centered on the fundamental shift in consciousness that is needed for a new paradigm to emerge, like our understanding of "energy" or "time," for instance. There are short, easy-to-read explorations of the interrelated concepts in each chapter. At the end of each chapter, I offer a short practice called Perceptual Mode, which invites you to shift your consciousness inward so that you can integrate the concepts in the chapter you just read. You might choose to keep a journal close, so you can write a little after each chapter to process the insights that arise through these practices.

# Part 1
# FOUNDATIONS

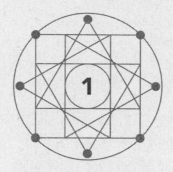

# PATHWAYS:
# THE POWER OF DIRECTION

*You have brains in your head. You have feet in your shoes.*
*You can steer yourself any direction you choose.*

DR. SEUSS, AUTHOR

## Your Magic Is Already inside of You

I wrote this book to help you adopt a new view of the world, create a new paradigm to make sense of how and why things are the way they are, and perceive how everything is interconnected. I will show you how the various domains of your life (like relationships, creativity, wealth and money, career, emotions, energy, and so on) connect with and condition one another. And how *you* actually play

3

a central role in generating your experience of a particular reality, leading to who
and what shows up in your life. Because
everything is connected, change in one
domain becomes a catalyst for change
in the other domains, and change in any
domain reflects your growth in awareness
and capacity. So, even though you might not
instantly understand everything you are
reading right away, or perhaps you don't see
what it has to do with you or your life, trust
that everything I am presenting to you will eventually lead to an
all-encompassing new belief system that will support your own magic,
your capacity to create the experiences in your life that you want.

Your life is part of a reality that is much larger than the obvious
physical aspects of it, and you can understand this reality through
modes of consciousness you already possess. Because we rely so heavily on the 3D modes of consciousness that we use so effectively, we
don't recognize other modes of consciousness that are also part of
our human inheritance. Our success in 3D makes multidimensionality invisible to us, as if it were behind a veil. As the alleged "veil"
between the mundane world and the world of Spirit is now dissolving, we are starting to realize that it was never really physically there
to begin with; it was merely an illusion brought on by our own state
of (un)consciousness.

Everyone has access to intuition, insight, and awareness that allows
them to comprehend and shape energy. You are more than just your
physical aspects. And those parts that are outside the physical realm
play a much larger role in how your life is unfolding than you might
be aware of. By comparison, the physical world is but a tiny part
of the vast and unlimited realm of the subtle and multidimensional
world, and we are now just starting to begin to understand this. We

are also now just starting to understand that our consciousness is key to accessing this unknown territory. And that within this multi-dimensional realm lies the power to our magic.

Once we come to experience ourselves as multidimensional beings capable of working outside of three dimensions with the multi-dimensional possibilities of the field, we can co-create our reality. This is what being a Modern Merlin is about.

## The Power of Now

To access and engage with spaces and places that are beyond our form-based, physical reality—to tap into a *multi*dimensional reality—we have to use our awareness (or consciousness) differently than what we are used to. Instead of focusing on the physical world, things of matter and form, like our bodies, our houses, our cars, work, other people, our clothes, and so on, we have to learn how to focus on what is present in the subtle layers of the larger reality that encompasses and transcends physical reality. The pathway into this realm of multi-dimensionality is intuition. Intuition can be described as an intelligence that recognizes patterns, apprehends energies that are felt before they are verbalized, and offers us a comprehensive, holistic understanding of our experience. It differs from the linear, logical processes of cognition that we use to navigate the 3D world. To tune in to intuition, we have to learn how to look inward and notice what information is coming to us in the form of thoughts, feelings, and images. And we have to be fully present in the here and now so we can receive the messages and insights that come to us.

So, before we dive deeper into this world of magic and mani-festation, let's take a moment to arrive, here, in this moment, with awareness. Something drew you to this book: perhaps you found it in a bookstore, or you came across it on social media, or someone gifted it to you. Whatever it was, here you are, settled in comfortably somewhere with this open book, finding yourself here on this page, reading this sentence.

As you will discover, being present in the moment might well be the most profoundly transformational concept to prepare you to participate in the new multidimensional world that is emerging. Where you are present is where you focus your attention. And where you focus your attention is where you direct your energy. And where you direct your energy is what you create more of. In short: like attracts like.

Perhaps you have noticed when the Universe responded to something you said? Did you perceive this as a form of magic? For example, you might have said to someone, "It's weird how I never see golden retrievers anymore; it's a shame, because they are such a loving and gentle breed," and suddenly they were everywhere you looked—on social media, on your morning walk, in magazines, on a lost dog poster stapled to a telephone pole, and in commercials during your favorite sitcom. It appears that the Universe heard your words and responded by bringing golden retrievers into your reality—a reality that is formed by what you are aware of. And clearly, you became aware of golden retrievers. And maybe what you were really longing for was the qualities you saw in golden retrievers: being loving, kind, loyal, and happy.

Being present in the now lets you become aware of your focus and your intention. That is the awareness that makes magic possible.

Your magic—your ability to create—works most profoundly when you are deeply deliberate and fully present with what you intend to create. That, in a nutshell, is what this whole book is about: like attracts like. Don't worry about fully grasping that right now. Trust that the journey we are on will slowly reveal all this to you.

So, that is where we are starting, you and I. We are going to make sure that we are fully present and that our attention is completely focused on this moment.

## Going Inward

Meditation is a great way to draw your attention to the moment. The purpose of meditation is to go beyond your conscious mind— the thinking mind—and allow your brain to slow down. The mind can be described as the brain in action, and this activity (in the form of brain waves) can be measured. When you are active, working, doing stuff that draws your attention to the outer world, your brain waves are faster than when you are resting, sleeping, or meditating. When your brain waves slow down, the rest of your body gets a chance to relax, rest, heal, and rejuvenate. This is also how you can tune in to the subtle layers of reality. By slowing down your thinking mind and moving beyond all the thoughts, the dos and don'ts, the shoulds and shouldn'ts, and the chatter of your mind, you can listen to what is "hiding" in the silence and the world of subtleties.

Unlike what many people think, you don't need to go to the woods or sit on a mountaintop to look inward; you can meditate wherever you are. All it takes is for you to be intentional and to find a little space and time to be with yourself.

Focusing on your breath
brings you into your body
and into the present
moment.

7

As we saw, to access our magic and be deliberate in what we create, we have to arrive in the present moment and become conscious of the subtle and multidimensional layers of our reality. So, we are going to draw our attention to the now moment by venturing inward.

Have you ever noticed that almost all meditations start with the invitation to take a deep breath?

Have you ever wondered why?

So, just put the book down for a moment, right now, and try it. Close your eyes, take a few deep breaths, and deliberately focus on your experience of breathing.

How was that? Did you think about anything else besides your breath? Even if you did, it probably disappeared a little into the background, while your awareness of your breath was *right there*. What did you perceive about your environment while you focused on the experience of breathing? Where did you "go"?

Have you ever thought about what happens when you close your eyes?

The most obvious answer would be that it gets dark, right? And this is true. What is also true is that by closing your eyes you shut out the outside world, blocking your eyes from seeing out there. Instead, you are inviting your eyes to see *in here*. You are directing your attention to the world inside you, drawing all your awareness and energy inward and into the present moment. Focusing on the movement of your breath also helps you direct your attention inward: your own breath becomes the focal point of your attention.

## Perceptual Mode

When you are *doing* something—like working on a project, taking a workout class, cooking a meal for your family, shopping for groceries, or driving your car—your attention is with what you're doing and often with what you have done, could have done, and might do. Part of your attention is focused on the task you're doing; part of your attention is focused on whatever might have frustrated you or pleased you over the course of the day, or planning what you'll be doing with the rest of the evening. Usually, you are not really paying full attention to your breath or your body; you're not focused on the *now* that you're experiencing. Instead, your attention is on what you are doing and on the accompanying narrative of what has happened anywhere but in this present moment. We call that focusing *out*, meaning your attention is scattered rather than concentrated.

When you're focusing *in*, your thoughts are not wandering; you're not moving into the past or future unless you intend to explore that experience deliberately.

Being present in the moment doesn't mean that you cannot be doing anything besides sitting and meditating. You might actually be perfectly focused in the moment while you're washing the dishes—the warm water, the feel of the sponge in your hands, and the smell of soap could all keep you perfectly fully here, and in that moment of presence a genuine insight might surface in the bubbles. The point is that your awareness is focused, present, and inward: that is focusing in. That is bringing your awareness into the present moment. In this book I am going to call this Perceptual Mode.

---

# Perceptual Mode: the ability to go inward and access your intuition in order to process the information that is coming from the multidimensional world.

---

To fully take in the information that I am going to share with you in this book, and to learn how to become a Modern Merlin who uses your magic intentionally, you have to learn how to be fully present in the moment, turning away from distractions of the outside world and refocusing if your attention wanders. Switching to Perceptual Mode, focusing in, and being deliberate is how we can be fully present.

To learn how to switch to Perceptual Mode, I am inviting you to become fully present with me here, now, on this page, in this moment, to begin with.

## Tune In

Let's start by taking a deep breath. Perhaps pause your reading right here, close your eyes for just a moment, and take that deep breath while pulling your attention from the outside world inward. This will help you move away from a place of doing and come into a place of being.

Do that right now. . .

Now that you have closed your eyes for a moment, you might feel a little bit more present here with me, on this page. Let's take another breath while reading along. Allow that breath to be released from your mouth with a deep sigh. Feel free to pause your reading at any time to focus your attention fully on your breath for a moment. Remember that you are doing all this to become fully present in the *now*.

Notice how your body moves to the rhythm of your breath. Perhaps your chest is going up and down a little, or your belly is expanding and contracting with each breath. Soften your body into the chair, relax deeper into your breathing, and let the feeling of your breath and your body become one. Let a softness build in your center, where your heart is.

Take another deep breath, relax, and notice how that softness is expanding. Perhaps take one or both hands and put them on your chest for a moment to help you draw your focus to your heart. How is it feeling? Can you feel its beat?

With every breath, sink a little deeper into that softness radiating from your heart area. Let the feeling spread throughout your whole being, opening you up and allowing you to be fully present here and now.

Take another deep breath and let it out with a sigh.

Welcome to this moment.

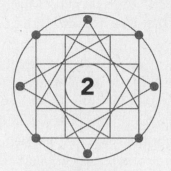

# MAGIC:
# THE POWER OF BELIEF

*How about a little magic?*

MICKEY MOUSE IN THE VIDEO GAME *FANTASIA: MICKEY MOUSE MAGIC*, 1991

D o you remember Mickey Mouse as the Sorcerer's Apprentice in the Walt Disney movie *Fantasia*? In this story Mickey is the apprentice to a powerful sorcerer. While his master sleeps, Mickey tries on the sorcerer's magical hat and casts a spell on a broomstick to help him fetch water. Unfortunately, as an apprentice, Mickey knows just enough magic to make something happen, but not enough to create the results he intends. In no time, out-of-control broomsticks are taking over and water is flooding everywhere, leaving Mickey in a complete panic as he tries to contain the chaos. Things only return to "normal" when the sorcerer comes downstairs and uses his skillful magic to reestablish peace and harmony.

# The Magic of Magic

Throughout history, humans have had a profound fascination with magic—and a deep fear of it as well. Magic holds seemingly unseen and unknown possibilities that can be of immense value, yet our lack of understanding and control makes us fearful. We assign great power to it, as described in countless fairy tales, myths, and legends in which magicians, sorcerers, witches, and wizards play significant roles. Merlin, Gandalf the Grey, Glinda the Good Witch, Luke Skywalker, Yoda, Darth Vader, Albus Dumbledore, Lord Voldemort, and Morgan le Fay are all examples of great magicians, witches, wizards, and sorcerers who have captivated our imagination with visions of what is possible when we know how to work with the unseen yet omnipresent energy of consciousness.

Perhaps our deep fascination with magic is our (often unconscious) desire to alter our existing reality, to expand beyond our current state and become a much grander expression of who we really are.

Without the belief in a possibility that things can be different—even if we don't see how—we would be stuck with what we have. This could rob us of perhaps our greatest force to evolve: our belief that change is possible from one moment to the next.

This book is called *Modern Merlin*, a tribute and reference to Merlin, a sage-wizard archetype for magic. He is associated with King Arthur, Camelot, the island of Avalon, and tales of times imbued with magic, mystery, and mysticism. Merlin inspires Arthur to imagine a Round Table, symbolizing the wholeness of the universe. Power is not reserved for one person at the head of the table because everyone has an equal role as co-creators of reality. Everyone around the table is charged with using their power to create a world that is fairer, kinder, and abundant in goodness and beauty. Merlin reminds us of the magical powers that allow us to alter our reality: powers we all inherently possess yet are often forgotten and dormant, waiting to be awakened.

Magic helps us believe
that anything is possible,
even the things that
seem impossible or make
no sense.

## What Is Magic?

Mysterious, fascinating, powerful, unknown, unexplainable, supernatural, impossible . . . all these words come to mind when we think about magic.

How can we describe what magic is? Perhaps what we consider to be magic is simply that which we cannot explain within the parameters of our existing belief system. The dominant belief system emerged from and has sustained 3D reality, so anything beyond what we are familiar with—like anything emerging from multidimensionality—can appear to be magic. If we haven't seen something before or we were never taught that something could exist, we assign it to the realm of magic and mystery even when we clearly experience or observe it. Or we try to force what is emerging from the new paradigm into the old box of beliefs and so deny magic, creativity, and ultimately evolution. Dismissing an intuitive child as an oversensitive one is an example of this.

Magic could be described as the explanation we give for something we perceive as real even though science has not been able to prove or explain it (yet) and our logic and reason struggle to accept it. The aspects of our intelligence that rely on logic, linearity, and the limitations of 3D reality may struggle to accept what cannot be explained in those terms.

What we know about magic from the movies is that it can make the impossible possible and the unimaginable happen. Moviegoers are expected to suspend their disbelief temporarily in order to enter the worlds created in storytelling and filmmaking. Consider how suspending your disbelief to perceive a new version of reality—for longer than just the duration of a movie—might expand your awareness and spark your own magical power!

## Magic is another word for manifestation.

There is probably already much more magic in your life than you realize. Amazing yet unexplainable things happen all the time. Sometimes these seem magical and mysterious, but often they are things we are used to, things we take for granted and have accepted as part of our reality without realizing that they are sourced from something beyond the 3D world and linearity, making them in fact *magical*.

For instance, think about the absolute bottomless and unconditional love you feel for your children, your partner, your family, your friends, or your animals. That feeling is undoubtedly real, yet it cannot be explained in scientific or linear terms, making it fall in the realm of magic and mystery. Other examples of things that transcend the 3D world can be God, angels, soul, connection, guidance, spontaneous remission, and so on. A lot of these are real for many of us, yet impossible to describe or prove in a way that fully explains the joy, comfort, guidance, hope, faith, fulfillment, and motivation they can bring us.

And then there are the experiences that "magically" alter the way you feel and therefore how you perceive your reality. They can instantly change your mood or your feelings about yourself, the world, or intangibles like "God" or "love." Music can do that. Some music can put you in a happy or romantic mood, and some can make you feel sad or angry. I'm sure you have experienced this yourself. Think about your favorite song. Why is it your favorite song? How does it make you feel?

Certain activities or experiences can instantly shift your mood as well: that first ray of sunshine after a cloudy gray day, a goofy puppy you meet on your morning walk, or a phone call from your least favorite family member. All of those have the "magical" power to completely alter your mood and therefore your experience of your reality instantly. Isn't that amazing?

Our inner guidance is another example of something "magical": very real for many, yet very difficult to explain or prove from a linear perspective. What I'm referring to as "inner guidance" are the insights and ideas that seem to come to us from out of nowhere, or from a Source that many refer to as a higher power, or from the Divine. Often this happens very clearly in the midst of seemingly ordinary activities, like washing the dishes, cooking, or gardening. Perhaps because our thinking mind goes into a lower gear while performing tasks that don't require much mental effort. Personally, my time in the shower often does that for me.

Of course, you can also deliberately access that inner guidance through mindfulness practices, like meditating or taking a walk on the beach, in the forest, or any place you feel closer to the Divine, like a place of worship. Our connection to the Divine might actually be our greatest expression of our (unconscious) belief in magic, as evidenced by the huge variety of religions all over the world and the sheer number of humans who believe in some sort of higher power or expression of the Divine.

Before we go any further, you and I need to come to an agreement about the words we are going to use when we refer to the Divine. Some might call it God, Source, Creator, Universe, higher power, Allah, or Spirit. I tend to use all of these terms interchangeably, as to me they all mean the same thing: my understanding of something that is larger than myself, that I feel deeply connected to, and that is guiding me through my journey here on earth. Some of you may understand the Divine or the Sacred in terms of a field of creative energy, a field of unlimited potential, or simply "the field." I hope you are comfortable with the way I use all of these terms at one

time or another and that you and I can agree on what I intend with it.

The paradigm that is emerging now extends our awareness of our relationship to the Divine, which develops through our experiences as embodied or incarnated souls. Many Western religious paradigms assert that the soul progresses from the body to an afterlife, which takes the soul out of embodiment and anchors it in a relationship with the Divine. The soul is uniquely expressed in a single human life, and whatever growth it experiences after death takes place as the soul serves God in whatever way is fitting.

The emerging spiritual paradigm seems more in alignment with the ideas of reincarnation that characterize many Eastern philosophies. It is possible to explore the insights of the emerging paradigm *and* maintain an authentic relationship with a religious belief that emerged from the older paradigm. This book offers concepts and practices to enable that. If your belief system does not include reincarnation, I invite you to find parallels in your spiritual experience that resonate with the insights I'm offering into old souls, our purpose for being here, and our opportunities for learning and contributing.

## Belief in You

Magic requires a deep and unwavering intent and conviction on the part of the magician. To arrive at that conviction, the magician needs to entertain a willingness to perceive magic as part of an expanded reality. Staying with habitual modes of organizing information in exclusively 3D and linear ways will keep any magician from developing the insight and tools to work with the Universe and perform magic. To see a world in which magic happens, we need to shift into Perceptual Mode, which allows us to go inward, access our intuitions, and align our creative power with the energies of the Universe and the Divine.

As we already saw, you can only enter Perceptual Mode through the present moment, through an experience of nowness—by focusing *in*. Focusing *in* enables you to perceive the multidimensional realm of subtle energies and whispers, where intuition recognizes the potential to bring into being what does not yet exist or to alter or transform what does exist.

To do this you need the conviction that focused attention and awareness brings you. The strength and stability of your conviction mirrors the amount of energy you can focus in the moment. The power you have as a magic-maker depends on your ability to direct all your energy into your intention. An uncertain and questionable "abracadabra" will simply not do. In the movie *The Fellowship of the Ring* (2001), when Gandalf the Grey stands up to the fiery Balrog in Moria, at the Bridge of Khazad-dûm—keeping the creature back so his friends can escape—and he needs the Universe to comply with his wishes, he shows up larger than life, grand in presence, unwavering in conviction. Imagine what this scene would have looked like if he had been uncertain, afraid, mumbling his spell and waving his staff in doubt. Do you think he would have been as effective?

Changing your reality starts with a deeply rooted belief that you *can*.

# The main ingredient of magic is belief.

Your belief that you have the power to change your reality starts with a deeply rooted belief in yourself. You have to believe in your own capacity to change the basic nature of your experience of reality.

You have to be absolutely convinced that you can change what is to what can be. This kind of conviction requires the belief that you can be in partnership and co-creation with the Divine. If you are going to change the way of the world and your reality, you have to work together with the power that created that world in the first place, right?

When you are deeply connected to yourself and to a higher power, your presence is without doubt. This solid connection is the secret power of all great sorcerers and wizards, who—based on their conviction, intention, and trust—are able to perform great magic.

## You are in co-creation with the Divine.

Let's look at *Star Wars* for a moment. The movies revolve around a mysterious power referred to as "the Force." What is the Force? How is the Force magical? How do you access it? What is required of a Jedi to connect to the Force and use it?

As we know, the first requirement of a Jedi (or a Sith) is *belief* in the Force and a certainty that it permeates all that is.

So, what is the unwavering conviction that is required of all magicians? That you're a part of the Divine. Part of Spirit. Part of the Universe. That there is no separation between you and a higher power. That you are in co-creation with it. That you are powerful. Unlimited. *Magical!*

# The Magic of Opposites

Every movie and story about magicians reveals a truth about all magic: magic depends on transforming one's understanding about opposites and how they relate to one another. Dark/light, good/evil, day/night, hero/villain, peace/war, and life/death are all examples of opposites we are familiar with. In our conventional belief system based on 3D reality, opposites are perceived as polarities in opposition to one another. This implies that they are in conflict or that, even when they complete a whole, they remain separate from one another. You might think of how night and day complete the cycle of a day, or how good and evil mark the extremes of a spectrum of morality, or how birth and death complete the cycle of life, or how ugly and beautiful mark the extremes of a spectrum of attractiveness or fairness. This is the magic of opposites in three-dimensional reality: things that seem to be in opposition actually create a whole, even though the parts of the whole continue to be opposites that define each other as separate qualities, experiences, or things.

Have you ever thought about what darkness is? How would you define it? Take a moment to think about it and give it a try.

And? What did you come up with?

Did you know that darkness by itself is actually nothing? Darkness is simply the absence of light. Doesn't that suggest something interesting about the dependence between opposites? About how we depend on seeing things in opposition to one another as a way of understanding their nature in 3D reality?

The 3D reality that we live in is based on duality, or polarity. Both words refer to the difference between opposite forces or qualities. You might wonder why we need both sides. Wouldn't life be much easier if there was only light and no dark? Only life and no death? Only good and no bad? Only joy and no sadness?

This might seem to be true at first thought, from within the habits of mind and perception that we've developed in 3D reality. From that perspective, we think that evolution or growth would mean that we no longer experience sadness, that death would be delayed or even conquered, that there would be only beauty, that there would be nothing to fear or worry about—no darkness or scarcity or loss. But when we dive a little deeper into it, we find some interesting insights that suggest another reality, one in which those differences are essential not just for our existence in 3D but for our evolution into multidimensionality:

## Day and Night

Our physical bodies are built to flow with the cycles of day and night. Our brains start making melatonin when it gets dark around us. Melatonin is a hormone that helps us slow down our minds and go to sleep. Sleep is needed for us to rest and to restore and heal our bodies. In contrast, when it gets light around us, our brains start making serotonin, a hormone that wakes up our minds and our bodies, so we can attend to our daily activities. These activities include the things we need to do for our survival and our well-being.

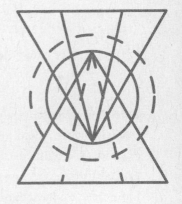

From within the 3D realm, we still yearn for only light, even though we understand that darkness has its purpose: we still judge light to be good and dark to be bad.

In multidimensionality, we make no judgments about the quality of each thing; we focus on the relationship between the two and what they make possible through the dynamic interdependence of their differences.

## Push and Pull

Life on earth itself depends on the dynamics of magnetics, the push and pull between opposites. Without the magnetic field that surrounds our planet, we would be exposed to dangerous radiation and our atmosphere would freely flow into space.

In 3D reality, south opposes north, and they are at odds with one another.

Our differences might actually contribute more to our growth than our sameness does.

In multidimensionality we perceive the field these opposites generate between them. From this perspective, in the interrelational context of magnetics, the push and pull between opposites is often crucial for the success of relationships that help us grow and evolve. I am sure you have experienced relationships in which the differences between two people actually contributed greatly to the success of the relationship. The push and pull does not tell us we are separate; it reminds us that we are each part of one whole: the duality of you and me becomes the nonduality of us.

## Life and Death

The cycle of life and death is at the core of all life. Life itself demands movement and change to perpetuate itself. The old simply has to die to make room for the new to be born. Still, in 3D thinking we want to eradicate death if we can, and certainly delay it—and all evidence of aging. We are afraid that we will end with the death of our physical bodies. Ironically, this 3D perception of death as the end of everything is what prevents us from living full and creative lives. If we want to re-create ourselves as fuller, more realized versions of ourselves, we must allow some aspects of who we are and who we have been to die in order to open space, release energy, and make room.

In multidimensionality we recognize that we are patterns of energy that emerge, dissolve, and re-emerge in greater complexity with each iteration. We are made of energy, and energy never ceases to exist. Instead, it takes on different forms. Our core essence, the soul, is infinite and will go on forever. So, instead of viewing life as a circle, which is the fullest 3D understanding of how the opposites of birth and death complete the cycle of life, a multidimensional understanding would view life as a spiral. Spirals are ongoing circles that never close but always take us on the next evolutionary round, symbolizing that life never repeats the same exact cycle twice. Life continues by evolving new forms, not just repeating old ones. Instead of dividing one life cycle into the duality of life and death, we recognize the nonduality of consciousness in which life and death emerge from and complete one another.

## Heroes and Villains

Where would we be without heroes? Much of our growth is based on a heroic quest to save the world or the damsel in distress. Wanting to do good, to make a difference, to leave a footprint or a mark is a huge motivator to improve ourselves and grow. Our evolution depends on it. Without darkness, evil, or wrongness, what would drive us to grow or change?

In 3D thinking, the drive is to eradicate darkness, triumph over evil, and allow absolute good to defeat absolute bad. Winning this "war" depends on the separation of light and dark, on duality, so that light can triumph. While *Star Wars* begins in 3D thinking, with Darth Vader trying to eradicate the light and Luke trying to eradicate the dark, the saga continues to a fully multidimensional epiphany: we all come to perceive the limitations of duality and the creative power of nonduality. In the end, good and evil don't battle to the death; they engage in a complex dance that releases the creative potential of both elements of the Force.

Not only is our physical reality created on the principles of opposites, but we learn and understand ourselves through differences. If we were all the same, how would we know what we liked or didn't like? What we wanted to be or didn't want to be? The choices that we make each and every moment determine the direction we take our lives. We learn about ourselves and the world around us through differentiation. But that doesn't mean we have to define ourselves as better-than or less-than; each of us is fully and uniquely part of a larger whole. We know ourselves in relationship to that larger whole, rather than through comparisons or competitions with others.

In the 3D realm, we unconsciously agreed to create a physical reality based on opposition. We have understood our relationships in terms of opposites in conflict rather than seeing them dancing as complements. In the multidimensional world, differences are creative and generate a common reality that allows everyone to realize their potential (making it real).

Think about rainbows for a moment. They wouldn't be the same if instead of the many colors they consisted of only one, would they?

The magic happens because of how all the colors show up as their own individual expressions within the spectrum of visible light and create a symphony together. Just like with people.

## The Magic of Complements

We saw how our Universe is created around the concept of opposites. Without this, life as we know it would simply not exist. Now let's go a little deeper and look at how, within a 3D Universe that operates through duality and polarity, there is room for merger, compromise, co-creation, and relationship in multidimensionality.

## Magic belongs to the realm of multidimensionality.

Let's go back to *Star Wars* to explore these ideas, just because it is such a fun and clear representation of a polarity-based universe that gives rise to captivating adventures, moralizing dilemmas, relatable situations, and tons of heroes, damsels in distress, and worlds on the verge of annihilation.

In the *Star Wars* movies, the Force inhabits all of us. How we choose to express it, *without denying any aspect of it*, is what makes us unique, what makes us ourselves and no one else. That's the lesson of *Star Wars: The Rise of Skywalker*: only by accepting that we are all Palpatine (dark) and Skywalker (light) can we access the full creative potential of the Force. Darth Vader dies as Anakin Skywalker because of the choice he makes at the end of his life. His grandson Kylo Ren chooses as bravely, and he and Rey, one-time enemies who wed the light and dark sides of the Force through their love, open the new reality of creative complements for everyone to experience.

*Star Wars* gives us perfect ingredients to help us question our own morals, beliefs, and motives, to see their limitations when we enact them as if all reality were found in 3D. It helps us learn about ourselves by presenting us with situations and questions that we can apply to our own lives as we explore multidimensionality. Who wouldn't want to have a cool lightsaber attached to their hip while walking down the street? Who wouldn't feel more whole in a 3D world when their vision includes multidimensionality?

Of course, there is a dark side and a light side of the Force, yet things are not always as simple as choosing one side or the other. We witness a constant push and pull between our heroes and villains to remain loyal to their "side" and their beliefs. We, as the observers, find ourselves alternating between feeling sympathy and hostility for both. In multidimensional reality, we (as observers) recognize that both light and dark are in us; we understand both and express the energies that characterize both, as we need those energies to create our reality and co-create the Universe.

With *Star Wars* in mind as an example of both the opposites and the complements that are the basis of the Force—and all magic—take a look at the images on the next page.

How do you think the images represent models of opposites or complements? What do you think each version could be symbolic of? What does the line mean? How about the dots?

Contemplate for a moment how these figures can represent relationships. Perhaps bring to mind one or two important relationships in your life and contemplate which figure represents them best and why. Which figure would you most prefer? What is needed to have a figure 3 kind of dynamic in a relationship?

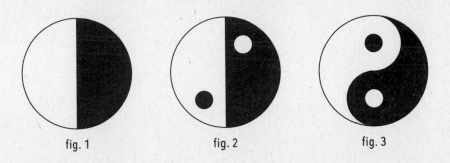

fig. 1                    fig. 2                    fig. 3

Magic and manifestation—our ability to co-create our reality—requires merger, compromise, collaboration, and the dynamic relationship of opposites. A dance that transcends perceived separations of polarity generates a magical wholeness.

# Belief

Belief is one of the most powerful driving forces toward action and change.

Belief can be described as the state of mind we experience when we think something is true. Up until recently, it has mostly been our conscious (analytical) minds that determined whether or not we believe something. If we found enough evidence (logical and scientific facts) in support of a thing, we would consider it to be true and, therefore, believe it.

In the new energy that is increasingly more multidimensional, it is no longer enough to rely solely on our analytical and logical minds to determine our truths and our beliefs. Our analytical and logical minds depend on duality; they compare and contrast, separate this and that, and sort experiences into the past and the future even as we're observing ourselves in the 3D present (on the rare occasions that we do!).

Once we believe
something, we steer our
actions toward a reality
and life that support
this belief.

Now that our world is being saturated with more and more multidimensional elements (like memories from other lifetimes or dimensions, enhanced extrasensory and psychic abilities, and an altered sense of time, for instance), we need to change the way we think. Our experience of these multidimensional elements challenges the duality that logic and reason and even common sense depend on. If we are to access multidimensionality and work with consciousness, we have to leave behind the fundamental dualities of past and future and be in a present that is nondualistic, transcends linear time, and can accommodate both 3D reality and multidimensionality. We have to be in Perceptual Mode, even if the collective or common mode of consciousness denies that it exists.

Unfortunately, 3D science, anchored in dualistic ways of observing and reasoning, has not caught up enough to provide sufficient evidence to make complete sense of this multidimensionality. So we have to rely on other parts of ourselves—beyond the logical, conscious mind—to navigate this exciting new world. If enough of us take this journey individually, our collective experience will shift. Navigating multidimensionality will eventually become part of our collective paradigm and belief system.

## Coherence

We are discovering how crucial our hearts and intuition are—that they need to be considered as valuable as our analytical minds—in determining our beliefs. To thrive in this new energy as co-creational, multidimensional human beings who are in control of their reality, we must *believe* we are these beings, capable of perceiving and working with a reality that our current science and habits of thinking cannot validate for us.

Self-worth is crucial.

Changing our reality starts
with a deeply rooted belief
that we *can*.

We have to believe without a shred of doubt that we are powerful creators. Just as magic requires a deep and unwavering conviction on the part of the magician, we have to believe that anything is possible— especially those things that make no sense to our logical minds.

Validating our hearts and intuitions as we explore Perceptual Mode is an important first step toward a new paradigm and belief system that recognizes the multidimensionality of everything.

The next step is to find alignment between our hearts (the seats of our feelings) and our minds (the seats of our thoughts). This is how the linear 3D world and the subtle multidimensional world come together, through the harmony of the thoughts that are generated by our minds and the feelings that are generated by our hearts. Together they generate the overall energy tone of our beings. It is in this alignment, this coherence, that the power of our magic resides.

## Tune In

Since Perceptual Mode is the foundation for working with multi-dimensionality, we're going to use that modality to explore the information we've been discussing in a 3D mode. We've worked through some ideas about multidimensionality using the 3D framework of linear thinking; now, by contemplating those ideas from within Perceptual Mode, you can experience and find familiarity with modes of consciousness that we don't usually use in learning, since 3D consciousness sees learning as an intellectual task that's dependent on linear, logical organization and analysis.

So, follow your breath into Perceptual Mode and bring into your awareness the concept "knowing." Simply observe what arises in response when you say the word "knowing." You may see colors or words arise in networks or patterns, or they may rise and fade away; you might hear sounds, recall memories, catch echoes of voices or

music, or experience smells as carriers of memory. Don't try to organize, understand, or assign meaning to what emerges; just be aware
of it and of the feelings, images, thoughts, or intuitions that attend
the experience.

When you feel complete, when nothing new is emerging and you
have had a chance to absorb what has been presented, simply focus on
your breathing, then on your body generally. Come back into the 3D
environment.

You might want to journal about what you just perceived and
experienced so that you can refer back to it while you are going
through the book.

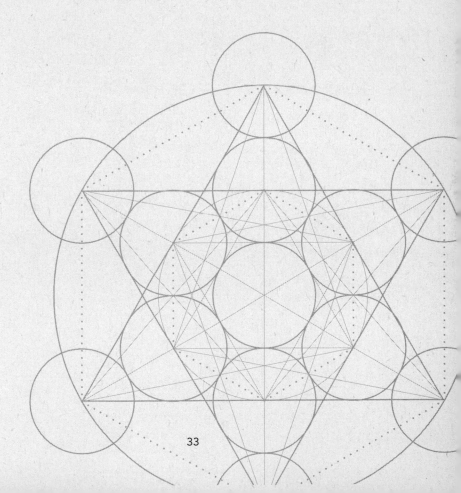

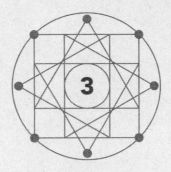

# REALITY:
# THE POWER OF UNDERSTANDING

*So far as the theories of mathematics are about reality,*
*they are not certain; so far as they are certain,*
*they are not about reality.*

ALBERT EINSTEIN, THEORETICAL PHYSICIST

## What Is Reality?

As part of the foundation you and I are building for a new paradigm, we are going to look at what we believe creates our reality. After all, if we are going to explore *how* our magical powers can alter our existing reality, we have to look at that reality itself first. What exactly is reality? Can we define it as an absolute or is it different for everyone?

Right now, think about something that is real to you. What is the first thing that comes to mind when I ask you to tell me something that is real?

How do you know it is real?

I asked my son this question, and his answer was: "that chair over there is real." I asked him what made it real and he said that he could see it, feel it, touch it . . . and even throw it!

To him, the reality of the chair was directly related to his experience of it through his senses.

While my son's example illustrates a collective definition of reality that is pretty straightforward, I am sure that if you asked a blind person to define how they know when something is real, their answer would be slightly different.

According to *Merriam-Webster's*, the word "reality" is defined as "the true situation that exists or something that actually exists or happens." This suggests that we can define a reality that is the same for everyone, regardless of belief, religion, gender, age, location, culture, time, state of mind, or physical or emotional state of being.

Let's look a little closer at the statement "Something that actually exists."

When does something actually exist?

When we see it? Hear it? Smell, taste, or touch it?

Those are all experiences driven by our five basic senses: sight, hearing, smell, taste, and touch. These senses are each connected to a specific organ in our bodies that sends signals to the brain to help us understand the world around us . . . a material, form-based, 3D world. This is a very important feedback system for any organism living in a physical body in a physical world. It helps us stay safe and healthy, warm and comfortable, and nurtured and loved. Our senses provide us with valuable feedback about the physical world that can prevent us from being burned, drowning, freezing, falling from a great height, or being poisoned. The information we get through our

senses regarding temperature, the elements,
nutrition, and our environment directly
relates to our physical bodies. It is real for
all of us who have a physical body. We
could say that this is a *collective* reality.

We are more than our physical bodies though, and our well-being and
happiness derive from much more than
just our physical safety and health. We are complex combinations of physical, emotional, mental,
and spiritual elements. In different esoteric circles it is even believed we
have as many as five or even seven bodies, including the physical, ethe-
ric, astral, mental, spiritual, emotional, cosmic, and Nirvanic bodies.
To keep things simple, in this book I will address the physical, mental, emotional, and spiritual aspects of our consciousness. While all of
these bodies are fundamentally the same for all of us—like our physiology—how they all work together to make up the complete beings that
we are, and therefore how we experience our lives, is very different
for each of us individually. Our collective reality can be very different
from our individual realities.

For instance, the coronavirus that became a global pandemic at
the beginning of 2020 was a collective reality, meaning that it was
really happening for all of us, all over the world. How we dealt with
it, how we responded to it, and how it impacted our individual lives,
however, was a *personal* reality. Even two people who both contracted
the virus and had similar symptoms more than likely had different
individual experiences; what was "real" for one might have been
completely different for the other.

For instance, while a body temperature over one hundred degrees
Fahrenheit is considered a fever for any of us, the way we handle it
and even the way we feel because of it can widely differ from person
to person. Not only does physical response, endurance, and reaction

to a fever differ from person to person, but emotional and mental response does as well. Some of us might address a fever only on a corporeal level (medication, supplements, nutrition, heating or cooling the body through environmental control), while others might use methods that are more holistic and include emotional or spiritual aspects as well (music, meditation, energy work like Reiki, crystals, and mindfulness practices). While the definition of a fever is a collective reality, each experience and response is individual.

## Not All Realities Are the Same

Some things are undeniably real for all of us: gravity, the ebb and flow of the oceans, the cycles of the moon, the seasons, the physiology of the human body, the wetness of water, the cold of snow, the heat of the sun, the 365 days the earth takes to do a full revolution, the fact that new life for humans requires a joining of apparent opposites (egg and sperm), and the universal experience that our current life starts with being born into a physical body and ends when that body dies. All these are considered *facts*: things that are proven to be true or accurate.

Everything we collectively consider to be true is what we consider to be real.

This truth is something we have collectively decided upon; as a result, we have made it part of our belief system, the foundation of how we understand our world and our reality.

Often these facts have to do with the natural world of living things; the physiology of how our bodies work; how we are born, grow, get sick, get better, and die; why the sun comes up, planets rotate, and stars appear and disappear; why water freezes at a certain temperature and becomes steam at another. These things are part of a collective reality that is absolute. They are true for all of us.

Then there are things that are part of a collective reality that are *secondary*, *relative*, or *conditioned*. They are real for all of us, but our understanding and experience of them might differ. We create institutions, ideologies, belief systems, and even economies and educational models to express the understanding of reality that we hold in common with our families, communities, coreligionists, or fellow

citizens. Our different economic systems, religious systems, govern-
ments, educational models, relationships, politics, and health systems
demonstrate this. For many people these seem as given and collectively real as absolute reality. They seem to have more effect on most
people's day-to-day life than the absolute does as far as their awareness is concerned. For many people it seems that nature is a backdrop
or setting for their experience, something they aren't consciously
aware of, unlike religious beliefs (if they have them) or consumerism
as a way to express selfhood.

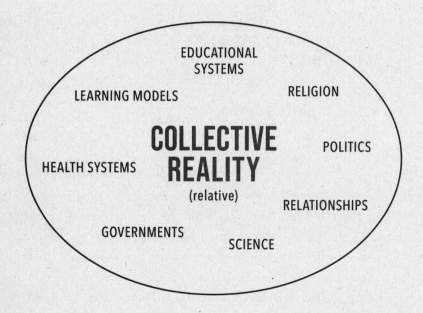

So, while some things are part of our collective reality—because
they are real for all of us, either as absolute or relative reality—many
of our experiences are personal and therefore create a personal reality.
What we perceive as beautiful, how we experience love, or how we
connect to a higher power are examples of personal reality. What
might be part of your reality could be completely absent in someone

else's. I am sure you can think of something that plays a big part in your life but is not present in the life of your coworker, sibling, or friend. While magic plays no role in reality for some people, for others magic is as real as knowing that the sun will rise again in the morning. Perhaps you are meditating on a regular basis and have experienced profound positive effects on your health and mood. This is very real to you. Your coworker, on the other hand, might never have meditated before. It is not part of their reality.

We could say, then, that reality is often not an objective absolute. It is simply our personal experience of our inner and outer worlds—the way we perceive them. Reality is different for everybody. And the reality we know is determined by the modes of consciousness we bring to bear in exploring it. If you're investigating reality using Perceptual Mode as well as 3D consciousness—if you've been using the practice we explored in chapter 1—you may have already begun to see how different your experience of the everyday world can be.

We all function within a bubble of our personal reality and together in a bubble of our collective reality.

## Reality, Beliefs, and Magic

In the first chapter we explored the connection between magic and reality. We found that magic has to do with our belief in our own capacity to change the basic nature of (our experience of) reality. We also found that magic requires unwavering belief on the part of the magician that he or she can change their reality. Belief is at the core of magic. What we believe or don't believe is paramount to our capacity to alter our reality and thus perform magic.

Many of these beliefs are firmly anchored in our collective belief system, either passed on from generation to generation or set there by our culture or religion. They limit our co-creative powers without us even being aware that things don't have to be that way. Changing our reality starts with believing that we can do so, but we often don't even *realize* that it is possible.

## A belief is a thought that you continue to think over and over, or a story you tell yourself again and again until it becomes your truth.

To change anything about our reality we have to become aware of what creates that reality in the first place.

Let's look at some beliefs in three general areas of our lives: the world, other people, and ourselves. Remember that what we believe to be true is what we believe to be real. And all the things we believe to be real together create our reality.

We are going to explore our "negative" beliefs, because those are thoughts that limit what is possible for us. They keep us stuck in our expression of who we are and what we are capable of creating. These beliefs block our magic.

## Beliefs about the World

Our beliefs have a profound effect on our reality. What we believe creates the possibilities and limitations of who we are and what we can do.

When we come from the status-quo perspective that "the world is not an easy place to be in" or that "danger lurks around every corner" and "the world is out to get us," we create a very different reality than when we come from a magical perspective that we are in co-creation with the world and anything is possible.

How do *you* perceive the world? What are your beliefs about the world and what is possible?

Often, we are not aware of the statements we make about what we believe. Many of us grow up hearing these statements and fold them into our own belief systems and thus our reality. The warning from a protective and loving parent about the dangers of the world might thus unconsciously become the foundation of our relationship with the world, limiting (or expanding) our ability to co-create with it. Becoming aware of the things we say and catching ourselves when we express beliefs that could limit our potential is a first step toward becoming powerful magicians who are in control of their reality. Instead of "the world is out to get me," think how that statement would change with the complementary—or magical—perspective. Something like, "I am a co-creator with the world" or "the world wants/invites my creativity."

## Beliefs about People

Just as our beliefs about the world have an effect on our magical abilities and our reality, so do our beliefs about people—especially the people in our lives. When we believe, for instance, that people are out to get us, men are only interested in sex, nobody cares about us, blondes are dumb, women are not good in leadership positions, people don't change, or intelligent people are nerdy, we will more than likely create a reality that reflects those beliefs. If we have negative beliefs about people, we might not pursue connection and collaboration with them. Thus, we limit our own creativity (and perhaps others' as well).

Think for a moment about beliefs you might have about other people. If you can't think of any right this second, pay attention in the next few days to what you are saying (or thinking) about others. It could be a belief about certain groups or categories of people, like women or men; children; Asian, Black, Native American, German, Dutch, Korean, or Japanese people; Christians, Jews, atheists, or Buddhists; scientists, artists, politicians, activists, lawyers, or actors; or short, tall, overweight, or athletic people. Once you start paying attention, you might find that we all have countless beliefs regarding just about anybody. And all these beliefs together make up your reality.

## Beliefs about Yourself

Perhaps the most powerful beliefs are the ones that we have generated about ourselves. Our self-worth directly derives from our beliefs about ourselves, and because our self-worth conditions our belief about what we deserve and what we can accomplish, it is paramount to our ability to be powerful co-creators of our lives, and thus perform magic.

If you believe you can't do something, that you are not good at something or that it's not meant for you, what do you think is going to happen? You might never try it in the first place, or you might try it and because you are so afraid that you will make a mess of it, you actually don't succeed and therefore fulfill your own prophecy.

Or you might try it once and if it doesn't work give up right away in resignation to what you already "knew."

What do you believe about yourself? What statements do you make about yourself and your capabilities? This could be something like "I'm not good at public speaking," or "I always attract a certain kind of person into my life," or "I would never be able to do what you did."

Most of us have countless beliefs about ourselves: opinions and statements that we have made part of our reality. Often, we are not even conscious of how large a part of our common language these beliefs are. Nevertheless, they can have a profound effect on our ability to attract and create circumstances and draw desirable people into our lives. By constantly emphasizing and highlighting our limitations in language we're not even conscious of using, we unintentionally strengthen those limitations.

If you are curious how many statements (both positive and negative) you make about yourself and your abilities, I invite you to take a notepad and make two lists, one that is titled "things I am really good at" and one that says, "things I am not good at." Try to come up with at least ten statements for each list. You might be surprised to find what you really believe about yourself!

## The Magical Perspective

The magical perspective refers to a way of looking at the world with a deeply rooted belief that we are in co-creation with it. When we believe that it is possible to alter our existing reality, we look at the world with curiosity, inquisitiveness, and wonderment, expecting magic and miracles to happen. This magic is multidimensional because it addresses things that are unseen, mysterious, subtle, and often as-yet unrealized—as in, not yet in our reality. It also anchors us in Perceptual

Mode in our everyday experience. In Perceptual Mode, wonder and curiosity erase the maps our judgments and ungrounded fears make for us, allowing us to explore new territory.

When we operate from a magical perspective, we can change the physical world and our experience of it. Think of how a statement about yourself would change if you used the magical perspective. Instead of "I am not good at public speaking" you could say something like, "I am good at public speaking if I act on my desire to connect with other people and trust that they want to connect with me and hear what I have to share." Instead of saying "I always attract the wrong person into my life," you could say "I always attract the perfect person to help me evolve and grow." All of a sudden, a limited potential—one that states that you only attract people who are not serving you—changes into an opportunity for growth and evolution: the person you attract will inspire valuable insights and opportunity for expansion.

## Three-Dimensional versus Multidimensional

Collective reality has mostly been defined based on things that can be experienced by the five senses and explained by science.

Because multidimensionality brings in the unseen, mysterious, subtle, and often as-yet unrealized, it has been only part of the personal reality of those who could access it through their consciousness. Since relatively few people have shared what they've experienced through their multidimensional consciousness, we've tended to label those people in ways that set them aside: as artists, psychics, shamans, or visionaries if we accept them, or as mentally ill if we can't. How many of us want to be seen as crazy or believe we are geniuses?

Now that technological innovation is bringing our understanding beyond what we can perceive with our five physical senses, we are collectively moving into a new and mostly unexplored world of multidimensionality. More and more of physics sounds like the descriptions of reality that shamans and healers have long worked with, that artists have tapped into, that creators who draw on intuition and inspiration have declared to be their domain. Our physical senses are not of much use here. We need to learn how to use a new sense . . . one that is not based in the physical. We need to develop our intuitions and our heart-centered perception to evolve, along with the world, out of 3D and into multidimensionality.

## Our consciousness is going to create the foundation of a multidimensional world.

To make this concept of three-dimensionality versus multidimensionality more tangible for you, imagine you're with a friend. They are telling you about something that is going on in their life. While your ears are hearing the words and your eyes are seeing your friend, there is much more going on than just the physical experience your senses are picking up. While your eyes and ears can see and hear that your friend is feeling emotional—happy or sad—you can "feel" your friend as well. Perhaps you even notice that you are starting to feel happy or sad yourself, as you are "mirroring" their emotions.

In addition, you are receiving lots of inner feedback while your friend is sharing their story with you—intangible, multidimensional qualities the five senses can't capture. Things your gut or your heart is telling you. For instance, you might be aware that your friend is compassionate, loving, and authentic. Or you might get the feeling that they are not telling you everything because you can sense some hidden anxiety or stress.

Often these multidimensional perceptions just come to us as a thought or insight. We just "know" without having any tangible indications or proof.

There is great value in recognizing that you can perceive others in 3D and in multidimensional ways. It can change the way you understand how others perceive you. Think of some situations where deliberately seeking this kind of feedback can be of value. How about a job interview? Or a first date? Or parenting?

When the feedback you are receiving is not just about what you hear, see, feel, smell, and taste but also includes what your intuition is picking up, you get a much more complete picture of the person you're with or the situation you are in. I am sure many of us have been in situations where our guts or hearts told us to get out—that we might be in danger—while there was no direct or noticeable (physical) reason to do so. The indication was "hidden" in the subtle layers of multidimensionality. We picked up on it with intuition.

Could this mean that we actually have another mode of perceiving reality . . . or sixth sense, perhaps?

## Turning Inward

To learn how to become aware of everything multidimensional— and all the subtle layers of reality—we have to learn how to receive that information. You aren't aware of all the subtle ways the Universe is communicating with you unless you tune in to the space where that communication is available, unless you enter Perceptual Mode.

And that means that you have to turn your awareness away from the 3D, physical world around you and go inward.

The outside, 3D world is often loud—not only sound but also the constant feed of imagery that comes to us. It completely fills our senses, demanding our attention in every moment.

To tune in to the world of multidimensionality and our inner guidance, we need to direct our attention inward. It might mean that you have to physically withdraw from the world for a little so you don't get distracted by the world around you. By turning inward, we solely focus on the thoughts that run through our heads, how and what we feel, the imagery that comes up, and anything else that catches our attention on the inside. We need to remember that Perceptual Mode is available to us anytime and anywhere.

## The language of multidimensionality comes to us through intuition.

In time you might find that you can turn inward even amidst the noisiest and most visually stimulating environment. Tuning in to your inner guidance and intuition will be your foundation for thriving in this increasingly multidimensional world. The more you can stay in Perceptual Mode even as you interact with the 3D world, the more magic you will be able to work in your own life.

# Shifting Modes of Perception

To strengthen this foundation, we are going to use images to enter Perceptual Mode, which enables us to access intuition and process the information it brings to us. The quiet that supports this mode of perceiving is inside you—you direct your awareness and attention to the multidimensional world of energy and subtle activity. We experimented with this in chapter 1; here we're going to refine and strengthen our practice. Your consciousness is like the beam of a lighthouse that reaches into the fluid and open space of multidimensionality, where information the five senses can't perceive is available to you. In general, intuition and imagination generate an awareness that allows you to perceive the potential that emerges from the darkness of unexplored reality. Intuition is receptivity and imagination is creativity, and together they reveal the gifts that are available to you when you open your consciousness to a larger reality.

You can enter Perceptual Mode whenever you want to access intuition or inner guidance to understand yourself or make sense of the world—when you feel like you need to rebalance yourself, when you feel sad or triggered, when you feel overwhelmed by life, when you can't think clearly, or when you simply want some time alone. When you use intuition deliberately to understand your experience of reality, your perception is less likely to be distorted by the beliefs that govern 3D, status-quo reality.

We are going to create the pathway to Perceptual Mode so that your intuition can speak to you clearly and you can perceive the world with less distortion. Perhaps this sounds a little strange to you, but because multidimensionality mostly takes place inside you, your senses are not going to be of much help. So just like your 3D brain creates neural pathways to process the information coming from your five senses, you need to create a pathway to your Perceptual Mode to process information coming from your intuition and your inner guidance.

# Tune In

Meditation is one of the most powerful tools to help us turn inward and go beyond the conscious mind, slowing down our active thinking and letting us tune in to what goes on inside us. And although many people experience incredible positive results from meditating for prolonged periods of time and on a regular basis, even the smallest effort to turn away from the outside world and focus inward can have profound effects. Just like muscles build with the repetition of a certain exercise or movement, our brains quickly adapt to new behaviors and habits and form new neural pathways that make slowing down easier and faster each time we do it. Scientists use the term "neuroplasticity" to describe the capacity of the mind to shape the brain. You might find that in time a quick five-minute tune-in can result in feeling as recharged as if you had taken a twenty-minute nap. Over time, you might find you wake up to a new brain, brought to you courtesy of your own mind!

Here is how you can do a quick five-minute tune-in. Read the following and then simply do it any way that feels good to you. Trust that you naturally know how to do this. It doesn't matter if you don't follow it to the letter; all that matters is that you turn your focus away from the outside and toward the inside, that you move your awareness from the 3D physical world into the world of multidimensionality. This is how you create and maintain your pathway to your inner guidance.

▲ Make sure you sit comfortably. This can be inside or outside, on a chair or a couch, on the floor or the grass. It really doesn't matter, as long as you sit in a way that feels relaxed and you don't get distracted by discomfort.

▲ Close your eyes if that feels comfortable for you. Take a deep breath. In through the nose, hold it for a second, and then out through the mouth. Do this again: in through the nose, hold it, and out through the mouth. Ahhhhhh.

▲ Now, instead of keeping your awareness right behind your eyes, as though you're trying to look through your closed eyelids, you are going to bring your awareness down . . . into your heart space. The way to do that is to visualize going down through your body, from your head into your heart. You are doing this to move from an outward experience to an inward one. You might get a feeling of going down or inward, as if you are taking an elevator down into your heart.

▲ Don't forget to keep taking nice slow breaths in the meantime.

▲ Now, keep your awareness centered in your heart space.

▲ Imagine your eyes dropping down to the center of your chest. You are observing from that space. By doing this you're shifting your perception from your mind to your heart: to your intuition, compassion, empathy, and non-linear understanding of experience.

▲ Allow impressions, images, sounds, or feelings to arise in this space. Simply observe—don't judge or name or label them (like, "I'm having an epiphany!"). If any thoughts come up, notice them but don't worry about remembering them or hanging on to them. Just have the experience of perceiving them.

▲ Stay in this space for as long as it feels comfortable to you.

▲ When you are ready, slowly come back to the physical world. Notice your heart beating or your breath going in and out to guide you back.

▲ Now, perhaps wiggle your fingers and toes.

▲ Slowly open your eyes.

You can do this at any time during your day, whenever you feel you need a little break, when you feel overwhelmed or anxious, or when you want to get a more complete picture of what is going on—not just on a 3D level but also from a multidimensional viewpoint.

Even when you are in the midst of something—work, a dinner party, a conference, a family visit, or a romantic date—you can always find a few minutes to excuse yourself for a bathroom break and simply practice your tune-in or pathway to Perceptual Mode. I guarantee you will feel different after doing this even for a few minutes, and you might find a completely new perspective on the situation you were in or the person(s) you were with. In time you might find that you don't even have to physically withdraw anymore; you can simply do it wherever you are, instantly.

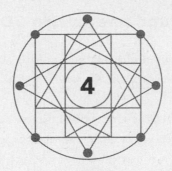

# TIME:
# THE POWER OF PERCEPTION

*How did it get so late so soon?*

DR. SEUSS, AUTHOR

Just as we looked at the concept of reality as part of our foundation for a new paradigm, we are going to look at time as a fundamental part of our 3D world. We will discover that time as we know it is very much of this planet only; everywhere else it behaves differently. In multidimensionality, time as we know it in 3D doesn't even exist at all, making it possible to experience the past, present, and future all at once. We will find that time does not behave according to linear or 3D rules, and our experience of time varies with our stage of consciousness. All this makes time magical.

# Fundamental to 3D

From the start of this book, I have been talking about the fact that we live in a linear, three-dimensional world.

Do we, though?

When we talk about the three dimensions that are at the base of our world, we are referring to the three options we have to physically move through space: we can go left or right, forward or backward, and up or down. These movements represent the three dimensions of width, height, and depth, often referred to as x, y, and z. If we describe where we are physically we can use these three dimensions to give our exact location in longitude, latitude, and altitude (assuming that we are on planet earth). This description and explanation of our reality has been the foundation of our world as we know it for a long time (ever since we discovered that earth is not flat but, in fact, a sphere).

However, if we apply only these dimensions to our daily reality and count on them to help us effectively navigate our lives, things actually turn out to be a bit more complex than that.

For instance, if you were to go on a date and you agreed on where to meet, with an exact location, all the right coordinates: longitude, latitude, and altitude . . . would you be guaranteed to find each other solely based on that information? Or would there perhaps be a crucial component missing? Sure, you agreed on the *where* . . .

How about the *when*?

You need to set a time.

Getting to where you need to go has almost become brainless and foolproof with the widespread access and usage of navigational apps like Google Maps and Waze; however, without the component of time it would be impossible to secure meeting and convergence, no matter how accurate the spatial directions are. You and I can agree to grab a latte at the hip and cozy coffee shop on the corner, yet if we don't set a time, we are not likely to meet.

So, although we are used to labeling Earth a three-dimensional place—meaning that most everything that is fundamental can be described in terms of width, height, and depth—it is actually inaccurate: our world as we understand it is founded on the three dimensions . . . *and* time. Time and our relationship with it are part of the very basis of our reality.

You could say that time is the fourth dimension to our three-dimensional reality.

So, in reality—our collective one—we actually live in a *four*-dimensional world. Three dimensions are simply not enough to accurately describe, let alone navigate, the world that we have collectively created. Time is as fundamental to our world as the three dimensions that we have decided to be the foundation of our reality.

Throughout the rest of this book, however, I will continue to refer to our world as a three-dimensional one. I choose to do this because although these four dimensions are inseparably intertwined with our reality, there are some differences in that the first three refer to spatial directions that are absolute, while time is relative. When I talk about our three-dimensional world, I am mostly talking about the linear aspects of it that are very much of the physical realm. Time does not fit in that description; it is very much of the magical realm, as we will soon discover. . .

# Time Is Relative

Time structures our daily rhythms—a time to work, to eat, to sleep, to socialize. Yet such an ordered concept remains relative (as we've known since Albert Einstein's work), meaning that our perception of time depends on where we are and what we are doing. We can interact with someone on the other side of the globe, and they can be in a different time zone (half a day or night ahead of or behind us), yet we can still share a moment together. This collective framework is created and consensual. A day may seem to move faster or slower, depending on whether we are at work, on vacation, or in the dentist's chair. Farmers may experience time differently than stockbrokers.

Einstein showed us that time, unlike what most people think, is not a constant. It varies depending on where you are in space and how fast you're moving. When you are on earth, time moves differently than when you fly around the galaxy in a spaceship. Einstein said, "People like us, who believe in physics, know that the distinction between past, present, and future is only a stubbornly persistent illusion." Just like reality, time is relative. How you experience time depends on where you are, how fast you are moving, and how you look at it.

## Time belongs to the realm of magic.

The way we have constructed our collective reality around time only applies to earth, and even here it is barely an objective consistency. In parts of the world we have introduced "summer time" and "winter time," or daylight savings time in America, meaning that we choose to turn the clock an hour forward or back depending on the time of year. We do this so we can make better use of the amount of daylight during a twenty-four-hour period. In some parts of the world we make this adjustment and in other parts we don't, making the time difference between those places vary throughout the year.

Think about this for a moment: the fact that we can choose to "change" time and how we perceive it shows us that time isn't an absolute in the first place. When we move our clocks an hour forward or back, do we really change time? Does the sun really come up an hour earlier after we move our clocks? Does the flower bud that was in the process of opening reverse or speed up its process? Are we aging an hour or getting an hour younger?

No, none of that. It is all about our relationship with time. Time is a social, sequential construct that society created to get a better grasp on reality—to determine when all things made of matter take place in our universe. It prevents us from experiencing things as happening all at once. And we divide time into three separate elements: the past, the present, and the future. This is a linear, horizontal way of looking at time. It's an assumption we've used to construct, organize, and order our experience in the 3D world.

There is tremendous value in perceiving the world like this. By taking the lessons of the past and applying them to our present we create a better future for ourselves. Our attention, therefore, is mostly focused on achieving the goals we set for our future. Horizontal time moves us forward, always with an eye on what's next, what can be better, and how we can grow and evolve, forever propelling us into the future.

## Vertical Time

Yet, now that we are waking up to the concept that we are multi-dimensional beings, we must consider a different way of looking at time and explore the concept of *vertical* time as well.

Vertical time happens when we arrive in the moment with all our awareness: we switch to Perceptual Mode and focus on what is present in the subtle layers. There is no consideration for the past, nor the future; there is only the moment and the tremendous richness it has to offer when we know how to perceive the subtle realms that are right on the outskirts of our awareness. We can find our connection to the Divine whenever we move our awareness into vertical time. In this dimension of time, we can experience God, the Universe, our souls, and anything that is outside the three-dimensional.

When we tune inward by attuning our hearts and minds, we start noticing information coming to us in the form of thoughts, feelings, and images. How does your body feel? Do you notice any places that hurt or feel off? Is your heart beating slowly or quickly? How do you feel emotionally? Are you at peace? Joyful? Stressed? Excited? When you close your eyes, do any images come to your mind? Or perhaps you are completely tuned in to the music that is playing? How is your breathing? These are all questions that can guide you to become aware of what is actually going on inside of you. It will help you to arrive in the moment, in vertical time.

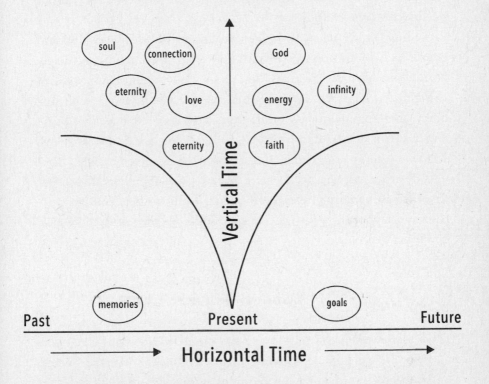

Often the outside world demands—and we allow it to claim—so much of our attention that we are not even aware of all the things our bodies are trying to communicate to us. And our bodies are the most powerful anchors to bring us into the present moment. When we become aware of what our bodies are feeling we cannot be anywhere else but in the moment. When you hit your toe against the corner of the bed, when your stomach is upset, when you are struck by a pounding headache, or when you are so excited by holding your lover's hand that your heart is pounding, you are in the present, feeling what is going on right now, in this moment. You cannot feel pain or pleasure in the past or the future. You can have a memory of it in the past, or imagine what it could be in the future, but the actual feeling—the experience—can only happen in the now. You cannot breathe any time but now.

Tuning in to what is going on inside—both physically and emotionally—can provide us with powerful information and feedback about how we are truly doing, so we can adjust our ways of being and doing accordingly. When we are not in touch with our bodies and our emotions, we miss out on an incredible feedback system that can support us with everything else we are doing as well as what we want to accomplish. Instead of being occupied by what happened earlier, or what to do next, spend a few moments in vertical time. It can be deeply relaxing, offering fresh insights and perspectives and supporting us as we move through our days with more ease and inner peace.

## Lost in Time

Have you ever felt you "got lost in the moment"? Perhaps when you and your partner were looking into each other's eyes, or when you turned inward to have a moment with God, the Universe, or the Divine? Or when you were creating a painting, sculpture, poem, or book that brought your vision into the world? Moments can easily turn into minutes and minutes into hours when your focus turns away from the outside world. Or it can happen the other way around: when you get lost inside yourself and are having a profound and deeply transformative experience, you might find that what seemed to be an hour in the depth of your being was in fact only a few minutes when you emerged back into the outer world.

Getting lost in the moment refers to the perception that time no longer exists.

When we switch to Perceptual Mode we enter vertical time. We can enter this mode at will, and it is available to us at any present moment. There is no need for a fixed and limiting attachment to the past or future, because we always have access to the vertical at any point along the horizontal. Getting stuck in the past ruminating on an experience, or fixating on the future by worrying or stressing, means you're split between the past (or future) and the present. Because you're not fully in the present, you can't access the *now*.

## Living in the "now" is paramount to living in multidimensionality.

Our sense of fulfillment, harmony, and (inner) peace in a world that we increasingly perceive as multidimensional depends on our ability to be fully present in the "now."

Our presence in the moment provides a solid foundation in which we can anchor our personal reality. This is important because the multidimensionality that is increasingly saturating our reality brings in complex and infinite layers of subtle energy. It would be easy to "get lost" in these layers without a strong anchor or reference point. Our present—or now—moment provides this anchor. By continuously bringing our awareness and focus back to the moment, we ensure a strong foundation for our physical reality. We experience our physical bodies in this physical reality, and paradoxically and magically our body is that anchor into the now (a very immediate experience of the complementarity that is part of multidimensional reality). If we allowed our awareness to venture into the field of unlimited potential without any restraints, it could literally be . . . infinite and unlimited. Without an anchor, a reference, or a boundary, anything would be possible, forever, limitless and endless. We would simply get lost in infinity.

By learning how to direct our attention and focus on the moment, we bring our presence back to here and now, where we can create the reality we experience in the now. Our bodies are essential to this process. We can do this, for instance, by tuning in to our breath or heartbeat and so bringing ourselves back to our awareness of our physical body. Our physical body is the 3D container that we occupy here in this lifetime to learn how to be spiritual (energetic) beings in a physical body. We are here to bridge the heavens and earth, to merge our three-dimensional world with multidimensional reality. The present moment is the point where everything starts and ends.

## Is Time Really Moving Faster?

Many people feel that time is speeding up. This acceleration can be partly attributed to technological advancements that allow us to do many things much more quickly and efficiently. We simply get more done in a shorter amount of time. In addition, many of us are constantly "multitasking," doing more than one thing at the same time. This often means we're literally scattered—our attention is divided and our consciousness broken up. We don't really multitask; instead, we switch rapidly between activities. More often than not we lose attention and energy when we switch, which explains why many people feel drained and exhausted after a full day of seemingly effective multitasking. What we call multitasking often accelerates our perception of time and even generates anxiety. Taking a break by exercising or mindfully drinking a cup of tea is not multitasking; it's a restorative and deliberate switch that lets us enter Perceptual Mode.

Another reason time seems to be moving faster is because many are finding their way to Perceptual Mode, learning how to turn inward and access the world of subtle energies and multidimensionality. Getting lost in vertical time in Perceptual Mode can greatly contribute to our sense of time speeding up in 3D. We have simply extended our range of possible experiences. Not only is our outer world full, loud, and complex, but our inner world is opening up to us and providing us with rich, deep, insightful, transformative experiences. To merge these outer experiences and inner experiences in a harmonious blend requires a whole new level of being and doing. It requires us to be Modern Merlins, contemporary magicians who are mastering the art of deliberate manifestation by working in both the outer (physical) world and the inner (multidimensional) world, sustaining Perceptual Mode as we journey through 3D "reality."

## Construct of Our Lives

"Time" is a huge part of our lives. You might not even be aware of how much it is woven into your language and the way you construct your life. Just for a moment, think about the sayings we use all the time (no pun intended) about time. *Time is money. Time flies when you're having fun. Time heals all wounds. Time stood still.* In addition, we (unconsciously) make statements about our *relationship* with time. Here are just a few examples:

▲ I don't have time for that right now.

▲ It's that time of the day / week / month.

▲ Every time I go there this happens to me.

▲ What a waste of time.

▲ I never have enough time.

Our approach to time often is a direct reflection of our sense of scarcity or abundance in general. Many of us are in a constant state of time scarcity, always running around like the white rabbit in *Alice in Wonderland*, proclaiming that we are running out of time (even if we don't know where we are running to). We feel a constant urgency to do more, do it faster, do it better. It feels like we are never "done"; there is always something or someone else to attend to, and it is never enough. And we simply don't have enough time to do it all.

Or do we?

A three-dimensional world is a linear world where things move from past to present to future. In this world, we are goal oriented, meaning we focus on something in the future that we want to achieve, something we don't have right now. With that goal in mind we set a direction and determine a plan of action, and we build our daily lives accordingly. And although goals are imperative to propel us forward on the path through our lives, our personal growth and evolution are determined and enriched by our journey *inward*, when we arrive fully in the moment and time opens up vertically. We then can journey into the subtle layers of reality, access our connection to a higher power, and develop our ability to translate the language in which the Universe is communicating with us.

Take a moment to explore your overall sense of time. Do you feel like you have an abundance or a scarcity of time? Or perhaps you always have just enough? Look around. Does the world right now seem to have an abundance or a scarcity of time? Has it changed over time?

## Meditation and Time

What happens with time and our perception of it when we meditate, when we perceive our experience using Perceptual Mode? Remember that we described meditation as a way to go beyond your conscious mind—the thinking mind—and allow your brain to slow down. When this happens, you arrive in the present moment, turn inward, and access the realm of multidimensionality. There is no time in multidimensionality. There is potential, energy, and infinity. In multidimensionality the past, the present, and the future are all one; it is only in the 3D realm that they are separated by the concept of time.

When we are in deep meditation and our brain waves have slowed down, we are in a no-time space. Perhaps you have experienced this? Even in a short amount of (linear) time here we can have the experience of eternity. When we are no longer limited by our physical body or a physical world, we can enter the world of multidimensionality through our consciousness and become infinite, limitless and eternal. Because this space is not three-dimensional, the laws of three-dimensionality do not apply here, making magic and miracles possible. I am sure you have heard some of the countless stories of spontaneous remission that people have experienced during and after deep meditative states. We are only now starting to touch upon what is possible when we enter the realms of multidimensionality, when we go outside the boundaries of three dimensions and time and allow potential to become reality.

# Tune In

Before you go into Perceptual Mode, contemplate or journal along the horizontal timeline three memories of times you felt connected to something larger than yourself. This could be a moment where you were standing in nature and you suddenly felt completely connected to everything, or maybe when you witnessed the birth of your child you felt you were part of a cycle of life that extends beyond your own . . .

Choose the memory of the event that has the strongest feeling associated with it, and recall (or describe) your sense of that experience in as much detail as you can. Focus on sensory, emotional, and intuitive feelings. This could be "I felt filled with light," or "I felt like I saw everything in greater detail," or "I could hear things more distinctly."

Take that feeling into Perceptual Mode and use that event as an anchoring point. Imagine traveling upward and inward from that point.

Open your awareness to any feelings, images, sounds, or memories that arise. Note that these are all emerging from one point along the horizonal timeline and are present all at once in vertical time.

Allow your awareness to enlarge, to hold all this experience.

If you journal about this experience, note what it felt like to drop out of horizontal time and into vertical time. With practice, do you feel you could enter vertical time at any point during your experience of horizontal time?

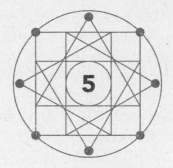

# ENERGY:
# THE POWER OF CONSCIOUSNESS

*If you want to find the secrets of the universe,*
*think in terms of energy, frequency, and vibration.*

**NIKOLA TESLA**

We have now arrived at what may be the biggest shift in our existing paradigm: the acceptance and understanding that *everything is energy*. Now, that is quite a statement, right? Don't worry about whether you understand or even believe that right now. We will get there.

We are going to look at how everything is energy. Everything. The stuff around you is, you are, your body is, your thoughts are— even your words are energy. A mixture of all of them together creates an energetic field around you. And *you* are the conductor of this whole energetic orchestra. But instead of being separate from this orchestra, you are a part of it as much as it is a part of you.

# Newton, Einstein, and Quantum Stuff

Back in the early 1600s, scientists began working with the belief that matter belongs to the realm of science, and everything else—including our minds—to the domain of religion. The philosopher and scientist Descartes even went so far as to say that *we are because we think*: cogito ergo sum. Nearly a hundred years later, Sir Isaac Newton stated that everything is made of solid matter. In his universe, everything could be calculated and predicted. Mind had nothing to do with matter, and energy was an outside force. For a long time, this determined how we understood the world: there was a total separation between energy and matter, soul and body, mind and brain, the perceiver and the perceived. Then, about two hundred years after Newton's foray into a science of matter, Albert Einstein took these theories even further (with the help of new technology) and found that time and space are relative, not absolute. He discovered that energy and matter are related, another example of the complementarity that characterizes multidimensionality. If you pursue one perspective on reality far enough, you find that energy becomes matter and matter becomes energy. You see that matter and energy are so dependent on one another in a complementary relationship that they are, in fact, one thing.

When technology got so sophisticated that we were able to observe the world on a subatomic level, things got downright bizarre. Physicists found that, actually, *nothing* is fixed or solid, that in fact, *everything* is made of energy. And that energy does not behave according to Newtonian principles, meaning in linear and predictable ways. They found that energy can manifest as a wave of probability in one moment and as a solid particle in the next. And what determines how energy behaves? We do! Yes, that's right:

## Our attention can change the way energy behaves!

What we think, where we focus our attention, what we expect, what we believe, and what we say out loud—all of it matters (as in, can *become matter*, become "real").

That, by itself, is pure magic, isn't it?

Think about how sorcerers, wizards, and magicians use words and spells to command the Universe to their wishes. They understand— consciously or unconsciously—that everything is energy and therefore all connected; they know you can use words to change reality by directing how energy expresses itself in matter. They also understand that the more energy you put toward what you're doing, the more powerful your magical manifestation abilities are. If you want something, *really* want something, you will have to put all your energy toward it. You are going to have to feel it with an unwavering desire in your heart, a burning passion in your soul, in every cell of your body and every fiber of your being. That's how complete your attention can be. And that's when you are most powerful.

When you draw all your attention inward and shift into Perceptual Mode, you experience your reality in the layers of subtle energy. You can align your desire, vision, and creative power to manifest what you have intuited as possible and imagined as real. You then enter the realm of multidimensionality and the space of unlimited potential. There, your ability to perceive possibility enables you to choose what your reality will be.

Let's take a closer look at how this works.

## Everything Is Made of Energy

So, it turns out that everything is made of energy. *Everything.* The whole universe is made of nothing but waves and particles of energy. An easy way of comprehending this is to think of the ocean. It's a vast body of water. Think of all the drops of water as particles forming the ocean. Now, there are different currents and waves in the ocean. While a wave is made of the same water as the ocean, not all of the ocean is a wave, correct? So, a wave in the ocean is made up of some sort of pattern that makes it a wave. Waves are made of particles in a pattern. This is the same for energy. All energy exists in a vast ocean of particles and waves. And all these particles and waves are moving, flowing, and interacting.

Because everything is energy, it is easy to understand that everything is connected. Energy is energy; it all exists in the same field. The only difference is in the way it behaves.

Let's look at how energy can behave.

All energy has a frequency, measured in waves. Some waves are fast, some are slow, and then there is a whole spectrum in between. We are actually very familiar with a variety of waves. Some you have probably heard of, like Wi-Fi, radio waves, gamma rays, X-rays, ultraviolet rays, infrared rays, and visible light rays. All these waves carry different information and can be received at different frequencies. And so do your thoughts, your words, your emotions, your feelings, and your dreams. Isn't that amazing? It's all energy, *all* of it.

## The Quantum Field

The smallest amount of energy is called a quantum (plural: quanta). Perhaps you've heard the terms "quantum physics" and "quantum field"? They refer to the study of the really really small subatomic particles, the micro system. This physics addresses energy and the space in which it exists and moves, comes together, and reorganizes itself in new patterns and structures.

The quantum field can be described as a vast, invisible field of energy that is all around us and that we are part of at the same time.

Quantum physics offers a useful analogy for understanding how our thoughts, beliefs, and projections influence the macro-level experience (our everyday life) we share in the world we co-create. Physicists talk about the *observer effect*, which says that any observation, whether it's made by a piece of technology or a person, introduces "error" into the behavior of the event or system that is being observed.

Being aware of what we introduce into our experience—whether it's limiting or expansive—allows us to perceive more accurately what's possible, what latent potential there is in the macro system of the world as we experience it. This macro system is a constantly emerging, dynamic expression of the quantum field, which is a plenitude, the field of all possibilities.

Because we perceive and respond to our experience and the world through the filters of our beliefs, relationships, sense of identity, needs, ambitions, and desires, we introduce "error" into what we're observing—ourselves, the world, and others. Error, meaning that our perception is personal and therefore subjective. We respond to our "error-ridden" observations rather than to the objective potential of reality. The more we are aware of the filters we perceive reality through, the better we can perceive the possibilities offered to us in any situation.

Since the way we respond to the world and our experience—with our thoughts, words, actions, choices, evolving beliefs, and identities—shapes the world, we are always co-creating the macro experience we share with others. In the macro world (our everyday life), we experience an interplay of beliefs, ideas, relationships, and identities—our own and others'—and their manifestations in form.

The world of matter that emerges from the interplay of energy at the quantum level is our resource for creativity at the macro level. What we feel, think, and intend can shape reality, because how we think, what we feel, and what we intend shapes our perception of and responses to the reality generated by the quantum field. Our responses help determine what probabilities in the quantum field are manifested in the macro domain, in our everyday lives.

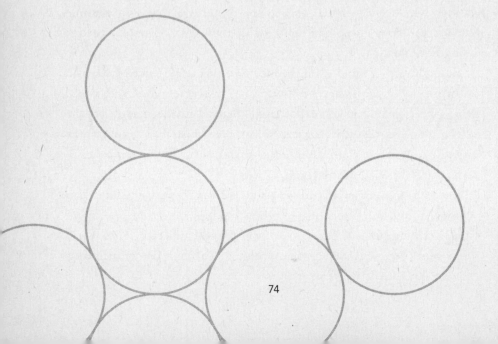

It works something like this: Every thought is a pattern of information that could be understood metaphorically as a vibration. Each of your thoughts has a specific vibration. Your thought about the color red has a different vibration than your thought about your cat. Or your thought about that chocolate ice cream you are craving.

Now, we have already established that there is an invisible (quantum) field around you, completely made of energy. All this energy is unformed and unmanifested. It is pure potential.

And here you are, thinking about the color red. This thought is pure energy, and it has the specific vibrational signature that states "red." You launch this thought into the field (simply by thinking about the color red), and the field responds to the vibration of this thought.

Now, the field is a plenitude of possibility, meaning that all potentials are already there. The potential of "red" is already in there somewhere. It is floating around as a wave of probability, waiting for something to interact with so it can collapse into a manifestation. Your thought about it is going to make it react. Just like magnets are attracted to each other, your thought about the color red is going to attract possibilities of red to you.

The energy in the field will automatically start organizing itself around that "red" vibration you sent out. It will try to match it.

You might find that you suddenly notice a variety of red occurrences around you. Perhaps you'll notice a lot of red cars around, or maybe you'll see a red flower, or you'll meet a friend who is wearing something red. Your "red" thought caused red effects in your life.

Of course, other people might be thinking about the color red also, and their thoughts and feelings are going to draw the possibilities of red toward them as well. After all, everything is energy, and all energy is connected through the field in which it exists. Everyone's thoughts and feelings have an impact on the field; they are interrelated, interconnected, and interdependent. What any one of us does affects the reality everyone experiences.

Our magical abilities derive from our awareness of the possibilities that emerge through our interactions with the field, ourselves, and each other. Since the strongest signal generates the greatest creativity (the ability to create) we need to develop our awareness as fully as possible—not just our awareness of the field's potential but our awareness of our own beliefs, purpose, and power as well.

# Like Attracts Like

The Law of Attraction states that "like attracts like." Our thoughts, feelings, and intentions are all made of energy, and we attract people and circumstances in our lives that are a vibrational match for that energy. We create experiences (organized energy) and things (organized matter) that manifest our thoughts, feelings, and intentions. Whether we are aware of it depends on our consciousness.

So everything is energy. You are, your thoughts are, your words and your intentions are. A mixture of all of them together creates an energetic field around you. It's your personal energy bubble, and it has a specific frequency. Imagine it like a radio station. All stations broadcast on a different frequency, like the news at 89.5, the latest hits at 93.3, and country music at 103.7. You have to tune in to that frequency to receive its programs. It works the same with everything that is an expression or manifestation of energy. Everything and everyone has a specific frequency. Using Perceptual Mode, you turn inward, opening yourself to the world of subtle energies, so you can tune in to different dimensions of reality. We can tune in to each other, the world inside us, and the world between us. We can tune in to messages from the Universe.

All this information is multidimensional. As we already saw, we can shift to Perceptual Mode and receive it. Just like training a muscle, we can train our awareness to tune in to the subtlety of multidimensionality. And just like training a muscle, repetition is going to be of great value here. The more often we shift into Perceptual Mode, the better we can perceive the possibilities emerging in the quantum field.

Because our collective reality is an expression of all the visions, thoughts, and feelings each of us generates, our ability to manifest what we imagine depends on the strength of our signals, the vibrations we send into the field. The more time we spend training in Perceptual Mode, the more we strengthen our signals, thereby increasing the probability that our visions will manifest in the 3D world.

By training in Perceptual Mode, we strengthen ourselves as multidimensional beings. As we become more comfortable perceiving the multidimensional possibilities of the field and more skilled working outside of the 3D realm, we increase our ability to co-create our reality deliberately and precisely. This is what being a Modern Merlin is about.

## You and Energy

Now that we have looked at energy from a semi-scientific point of view and explored what is possible and how (in theory) to make the possible real, let's bring the concept of everything-is-energy closer to your everyday life.

You might not be aware of this, but you are constantly exchanging energy with everything and everyone around you, all day long, and even all night and when you dream. You are made of energy—so is everyone else, and everything around you. Even your words, your thoughts, your emotions, and your dreams are energy . . . it is all one big dance, entanglement, and interaction between energies. Energy flows from you to everything around you, and vice versa. You are in constant relationship with your surroundings, and your surroundings (including all the people in them) are in constant relationship with you.

# People

We already saw that you, your body, your words, your thoughts, and your feelings all together create an energy field around you. This field can extend several feet beyond your physical body. Its essence is made up of all the thoughts, emotions, words, and intentions you have. When your thoughts and feelings are all happy, your field reflects that and is a happy field. When you are sad, anxious, and stressed, your field reflects that as well.

Now, think about how other people have their own energy fields that extend beyond their physical bodies, reflecting their thoughts, feelings, and emotions. So, when we are in each other's presence, our energy fields touch and overlap each other. The closer we get (physically), the more they overlap.

Looking at it this way, it is quite easy to grasp that we pick up energy from others. Not only do our fields overlap, but our energies also interact and blend. It's like pouring red paint into a container of yellow paint. The more you pour and the more you move and stir it, the more it blends. It is often like this with people as well; the longer we are in someone's presence the more we get entangled with them and how they feel. Have you ever been in a great mood and met up with a friend who was in a real funk, and after spending some time with them you noticed that your happy mood had vanished?

Of course, the reverse could happen as well; your upbeat and sunny demeanor could totally lift your friend up and you might find yourselves doing a happy dance after being together for a little while. Which scenario is more likely? It is hard to predict. There are no rules about this kind of energy exchange and interaction. This is very multidimensional, and so far, the realm of multidimensionality is one of magic and mystery. However, more than likely, the person with the strongest energy will have more of an impact. Just like the amount of red or yellow paint determines the outcome of the color mixture, so the strength and essence of your energy sets the tone for the mood between the two of you. In any case, being aware of your energy and its ability to affect others, and vice versa, is necessary for you to be healthy, creative, and happy. Accessing Perceptual Mode gives you that awareness.

# Empaths

Many people easily pick up on the mental and emotional states of others. They are highly sensitive to other people's moods and thus their energy. We call these people "empaths," derived from the word *empathy*, which can be described as the ability to understand the experiences and feelings of others. To stay with the metaphor of the radio receiver, an empath's receiver is highly sensitive, and they can pick up on even the faintest signals. Often, they pick up on other people's energy far outside their own field or bubble, so they don't even have to be that close to someone or be in their presence for a prolonged time. It can happen just by passing in a supermarket aisle. They can do this consciously, but more often than not this happens unconsciously, making it challenging for them to be around other people, especially crowds. They pick up on everybody's energy and that makes them feel overwhelmed. And often, they don't even know why they feel that way, let alone what to do about it.

Is this you? Keep reading! As the multidimensional world and all the subtle energetic layers become easier to access, we will need new tools for new ways of being and doing. You'll find these tools later in the book. There are easy ways of protecting yourself, and powerful tools that can be used to clear yourself of unwanted energies. They can easily be integrated in your everyday routines so you stay balanced and happy. In any case, these empathic abilities become strengths as you train in Perceptual Mode.

Is this not you? Still keep reading! Empathic strengths will emerge with training in Perceptual Mode.

## Places and Spaces

Have you ever walked into a certain space (like a restaurant, a store, or someone's home, for instance) and immediately felt that something was "off"? Without any clear or direct reason, you just didn't feel good there. You wanted to leave as soon as possible. Or the complete opposite: you walked into someone's home and immediately thought, "Wow, I love this place!"

Sometimes you can find obvious reasons that explain why you like or don't like a space. It could be the furniture, the colors, or even the way it smells, but sometimes there is no reason besides the feeling you have. You are picking up on the space's energy.

Since everything is energy and you constantly interact with everything and everyone around you, indoor places like homes, offices, studios, restaurants, hotels, and bars—but also outdoor spaces like fields, beaches, forests, mountains, and gardens—hold energy as well. Often, they reflect the energy of people who are there or have been there, recently but also in the past.

It is interesting to hear stories of sensitive people who visit places that are known for tragic events—sometimes even in the far past—and can feel the energy that reflects that. Or the many experiences people have with places that are haunted. Depending on our sensitivity (our awareness of energy), we can pick up on energy from others, whether they are still physically there or not. When we move into Perceptual Mode and access all the subtle layers in vertical time, we can pick up experiences and events from the past as energy patterns in our present moment.

We become especially aware of someone when they are physically close and their energy field partly overlaps ours. Just imagine for a moment that you are in a completely dark space, like a closet. Now, imagine that someone is with you in that closet. You can't see them because it's pitch dark. And imagine that you can't hear them, feel them, or smell them. Do you think you could sense them?

These are all examples of an increasingly perceivable multidimensional world. There is no place or time in multidimensionality, so no past-present-future, and everything is accessible at once. Evolution is opening more people to these multidimensional experiences. But we can be intentional about this and feel less unsettled or overwhelmed by them.

## Feng Shui

The term "feng shui" can be translated as "wind-water." In Chinese culture, wind and water are both associated with good health and good fortune. In the East they have understood for centuries that there is constant exchange going on between us and our surroundings, and that we have the capacity to bring harmony between ourselves, our environment, and the natural world. This understanding shapes aesthetics, spiritual practice, and relationships—relationships between people and relationships between people and their environment.

This belief system acknowledges that everything is energy, that energy is all around us and that we are in constant interaction with it. Eastern philosophy and science begin with the idea that ultimately there is no us and them, no either-or: we are interdependent with one another rather than in opposition to each other; reality is both-and. Reality emerges between us and expresses a harmony of differences rather than dualistic conflict between opposites. Therefore, it matters where we build our homes and businesses, how we build them, what direction they face, what materials we use, what colors we use, and what thoughts and intentions we project on our environment.

The art of feng shui is ancient, multilayered, and very complex. Practitioners often go through many years of in-depth training. There is a deep understanding of how intertwined we are with our environment and how important it is to build our physical world according to the same principles as life's creation. At the core are the five elements that form the building blocks of life: earth, metal, water, wood, and fire. In feng shui these elements are interrelated with facets of our lives. Typically, feng shui seeks to balance these five elements in your home and in each of your life areas (like relationship, career, health, wealth, personal growth, and so on).

It would be too much to go deeply into the topic of feng shui here; it is beyond the scope of this book and I am by no means an expert on the practice. For what we are exploring here—that everything is energy and that we constantly interact with our environment—it is enough to know that we can work with energy through the way we create our world around us, how we organize our material reality to reflect multidimensional reality. So, for instance, if a specific room in your house doesn't feel good, we could look at the balance between the placement of furniture, the colors, and the materials that are used. Perhaps your room needs more of the wood element and the simple addition of a wooden item could greatly improve the energy in that space. Remember that in the realm of energy and multidimensionality, things don't work in the same linear fashion as they do in our 3D world. Size, distance, and time are relative here. Because everything is energy, it is often enough to bring in something small that holds the essence of an element (like wood) to make a large impact on the overall feel of a space.

Although a feng shui practitioner could offer you valuable insight and services, you don't need to be a specialist to make small improvements to your space. Just look around and observe your space for a few minutes. How does it feel? Is there a lot of stuff around you? Is it organized or is it cluttered? Often, when we declutter our space, we instantly feel a sense of relief, suggesting that our environment is directly related to our minds. Is your space physically pleasing to the eye? Is there harmony between the colors? Do you have pleasing and uplifting art on your wall? Inviting and comfortable furniture? Does it smell nice in your space? Do you have plants or fresh flowers somewhere? These are just a few simple suggestions. Later in this book we will go deeper into how to work with energies and what you can do to balance and harmonize your space and surroundings.

## Living Planet

Just like we each have an energy field around us, so does every living thing, including our planet. We live inside the energy field of our planet. Therefore, we are intimately entangled with her energy; we pick up on her energy and she picks up on ours. A great example to illustrate this is the work by Masaru Emoto, who discovered our deep and lasting connection to water. In his research he uncovered that our thoughts and emotions have a measurable effect on water. He published dozens of images of water molecules that changed form under the influence of nearby emotions. Happy and peaceful thoughts resulted in beautiful mandala-like shapes, while sad and angry thoughts distorted the shape. When he implemented these findings in experiments with growing plants, the results were astonishing. Plants exposed to happy thoughts thrived, while the ones that were only exposed to sad and angry emotions withered away.

Considering how much our planet, our immediate environment, and we, ourselves, are made of water, it is unmistakably clear how much we are intertwined with both our inner and outer worlds and that our thoughts and feelings matter. . . as in, *become matter.*

Because we are so deeply intertwined with our planet, immersing ourselves in the beauty and energy of nature is one of the most powerful tools we have to maintain our balance and recharge ourselves when we feel low. I am sure you have experienced this yourself: how a simple walk outside, dipping your feet in the ocean, smelling the sweet scent of jasmine in the air, listening to chirping birds, watching dogs play, hugging a tree, buying a bouquet of flowers, or walking barefoot on grass can quickly change the way you feel.

# Tune In

We are going to do something similar to the tune-in in chapter 3 and expand it with some of what we just learned in our journey through the world of energy. We are going to combine our process of tuning in with our understanding of our relationship with our environment and explore how it can support us.

It is amazing how in a few minutes of leaning against a tree (with your eyes closed so you can easily switch to Perceptual Mode) you can connect to the world of subtle energies and tap into the powerful energy field that radiates from the trunk. You can enhance the effects of this experience by combining it with a visualization.

Let's see how this could look.

I invite you to read through what follows once so you understand the intention. Don't worry about remembering the details completely or doing it exactly as described, the most important thing we are trying to do here is to guide your awareness away from the outside world so you can connect with the energy of the tree, and through the tree with Mother earth.

▲ Make sure you are comfortable, whether you are sitting with your back against the tree or simply leaning against it while standing up.

▲ Close your eyes if that feels comfortable for you. Take a deep breath. In through the nose, hold it for a second, and then out through the mouth. Do this again: in through the nose, hold it, and out through the mouth. Ahhhhhh.

▲ Now, instead of keeping your awareness behind your eyes—almost like trying to look through your closed eyelids—bring your awareness to the tree. Just start noticing what the tree feels like under your hands or against your back, how strong it feels, how safe it feels to lean against it. Perhaps you are aware of the wind ruffling through the tree's leaves, or birds chirping away on its branches.

▲ Don't forget to keep taking nice slow breaths in the meantime.

▲ Start visualizing how the tree's roots reach deep into the earth, giving it strength and stability. These roots directly connect the tree to Mother Earth, where she provides the tree with the nourishment it needs to grow, like nutrients and water. Imagine how the tree takes in all this through its roots, pulling it up from the earth into its being.

▲ Now imagine that just as the nutrients are being pulled up from the earth into the tree, so is the energy. Imagine a constant stream of light flowing from the earth into the tree . . . and into you. You can make this light any color you want, perhaps a beautiful silver, radiant white, or warm gold . . .

▲ While you are being filled with this beautiful light, anything that you want to let go of you can allow to flow out of you. Imagine this as a different flow of energy streaming through your feet into the earth, where she will easily transmute this energy into the light.

▲ For as long as you want, stay in this space of flowing light while anything unwanted flows out through your feet.

▲ When you are ready, slowly come back to the physical world. Notice your heart beating or your breath going in and out to guide you back.

▲ Now, perhaps wiggle your fingers and toes.

▲ Slowly open your eyes.

▲ Give a silent thank-you to the tree for being the vessel for your connection to Mother Earth.

# Part 2
# YOU

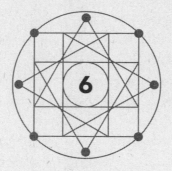

# SOUL:
# THE POWER OF INFINITY

*My soul is from elsewhere, I'm sure of that,*
*and I intend to end up there.*

**RUMI, POET**

Now that we have explored the foundations of our reality, we have discovered that, unlike what we've mostly been taught, most of these foundations are quite relative. What we thought to be solid (like everything in the world of matter and stuff) or absolute (like time) turns out to be nothing like that at all. It is all pure energy. And it is constantly changing and interacting. Our reality is founded on energy, and our consciousness is key. What a great discovery to continue our adventure with!

We are now going to look at everything that has to do with *you*. We are going to start with who you really are. The you beyond your physical body. The you who is an energetic being. We are going to explore the part of you that is larger than you and more akin to the Divine. We are going to look at how this divine essence in your core carries attributes and qualities that cannot be attributed to genetics, upbringing, or culture (the various programs that we run in our subconscious). What is it that makes you so special? Where did that come from, and how do you get in touch with it?

What is your magic?

## We Are More Than

We live in a time of rapidly expanding consciousness, and we are starting to integrate the concept of multidimensionality into our belief system. As we awaken to the notion that we are far larger than our existing paradigms have allowed us to believe, we increase our ability to communicate with and receive guidance from places beyond our 3D world. We are discovering that we are not only humans having a spiritual experience; we are spirits having a human experience. We are multidimensional beings, an energetic symphony of waves and particles, stretching through an ocean of layers of time and dimensions.

Many of us have a distinct feeling that we are much more than the people in the physical bodies we were born into. We often feel old and wise beyond our years. Sometimes we remember experiences, people, or places that we *know* weren't part of our current lifetimes, and we often feel driven by an unexplainable passion to fulfill a purpose, make a difference, and leave a mark.

For so long the Divine was presented to us as an outside source, something to worship and even fear. Now we understand that each and every one of us is part of that Divine as much as that Divine is part of us, reflecting the deep interconnectedness that characterizes the Universe. We are just starting to touch the tip of the iceberg of what is possible for us, how much power we have, and all the magic that is right at our energetic fingertips. Not even the sky will be our limit when we learn how to access all this magic in co-creation with the Divine.

## Got Soul?

Like love, the soul has always fascinated humankind. Some describe the soul as the spiritual essence of the human, that which is beyond the physical part. Others refer to it as the Divine in us, a little piece of God within.

While we are mortal as physical beings, the soul is considered eternal. Many believe that death is merely a transition in which the soul separates from its physical vessel and then returns in a new body. Although the belief in reincarnation is mainly found in Eastern religions, the belief in a soul is pretty much universal.

The soul is as elusive as it is mysterious. As much as we feel beyond any doubt that there is such a thing as the soul, we have no way of determining what it really is, let alone proving that it exists. The soul seems to be part of us, yet we don't know exactly what it is, nor where it is. Is it inside us, or is it outside? Unlike the physical, 3D parts of our bodies, the soul is multidimensional, everywhere and nowhere at the same time.

# The soul is another aspect of us that is from the magical realm.

Despite all the things we don't know about the soul, most of us have an intrinsic or intuitive sense of it. The word "soul" evokes thoughts of something ancient, something deep and mysterious, something that is us yet is larger than our human selves. Something that connects us to the Divine. In religious context, the word "soul" is mentioned as God breathed life into man. We are each born as a living soul; we do not obtain our souls from our parents. The soul is the part of us that always is and always will be. It's our divine essence, infinite and eternal. When our corporeal bodies die, our souls remain as part of the Divine.

## Heart and Soul

All this brings up interesting questions. If we have a part that is eternal and connected to the Divine, is there a different kind of consciousness attached to us as well? Do we think differently when we use our physical brain and 3D understanding of self than when we use our soul and its multidimensional perspective of a soulself? Is there such a thing as a "self" and a "soulself"?

I am sure you can come up with examples of times when your 3D-mind was telling you to do one thing, but something that was not your 3D-mind was telling you something else. Sometimes we attribute that to our hearts, sometimes to our souls, and sometimes we don't really know the difference. Perhaps the distinction between the two is that the heart can be described as the seat of intuition in the physical body, while the soul is the bridge between us and divinity. While both have multidimensional attributes, the heart is of the physical realm, whereas the soul is completely of the spiritual one. When heart and soul are attuned and we enter vertical time, we could say we are in our multidimensional minds. The heart is very much in touch with everything that has to do with this lifetime, while the soul brings the experience and insights of all lifetimes lived, or its experience of the Divine as a unique expression in this one life. Together they are a powerful source of insights and can offer us valuable guidance beyond what the mind has to offer.

How do you get in touch with your soul? The short answer is through Perceptual Mode. The longer answer is that we get in touch with our souls by going inward and connecting to the realm of multidimensionality and subtle energies. If the soul is larger than we are as physical beings, then entering into vertical time and allowing the moment to open up will give us access to the vast space of multidimensionality . . . and an experience of ourselves as souls.

## Old Souls

When we speak of "old souls," we usually refer to people who seem to have been born with qualities beyond their years and beyond what they learned in this life. Often, they are more mature and wiser than their chronological age can logically account for, or they exhibit a certain skill or talent that cannot be explained based on their age and experience. The old souls that especially stand out are children, because the contrast between them and their peers is so undeniable and profound. I am sure you have heard or seen examples of child prodigies who play the piano like Mozart, solve mathematical puzzles that boggle the "normal" mind, or paint like Rembrandt. There is no logical explanation for their mastery, as it far exceeds what should have been possible in the short number of years they have had to develop their skill. So, we pretty much have no other option but to entertain the concept that they were simply born with it. How is that possible, though? And what does that mean?

While many believe that the Divine gifts each soul only one human lifetime to express the gifts and qualities it has been endowed with, many believe that the soul carries the experiences of many life-times. Both of these are valid frameworks for recognizing that each of us expresses a unique energy, or soul, and that each of us has our origin in Source, which people refer to variously as God, the Divine, the Universe, the Sacred, Spirit, and so on. For those who believe in reincarnation, an old soul has been here many times, lived, loved, and learned throughout each life, and then taken that experience with them into the next lifetime. And they have greater access to the sum of everything they have experienced as a human: all the people they have loved and feared, the skills mastered, the lessons learned, the way they lived and died. Nothing is forgotten; it all is stored and carried in the eternal part that we refer to as the soul.

Often, an old soul's "soul age" is reflected in the way they show up in life and how they behave: calmer, more balanced, contempla-tive, reflective, not easily triggered, nonreactive, nonjudgmental, and very often with a clear vision and drive for what they want to accomplish and where to steer their lives. They often have an overall attitude of been-there-done-that and I-know-better. Have you ever met someone who felt like an old soul? What made you consider that they could be an old soul? Was it something in their attitude?

Did you look into their eyes? The eyes are considered the mirrors of the soul and can reveal the depth and layers of our consciousness and presence. Old souls often have mesmerizing eyes that seem to have infinite depth and clarity. It would be easy to get lost in them, or simply rest in their calm and compassionate regard.

I have always thought that it makes sense in a beautiful way, the idea that we are not merely humans on a temporal adventure for this lifetime, that everything does not end with the death of our three-dimensional corporeal body, that a part of us is multidimensional, eternal, a co-creator with the Creative Source. As we evolve and learn throughout our lives, our experiences become part of our multidimensional soulselves and carry through to our next visit to the 3D world or come with us as we transition into the next stage of life, the one that extends past physical death. This is part of our magic; we are a mixture of energies in many different forms. Some are solid and temporary (like our bodies), and some are subtle and multidimensional, and thus eternal. Like our soul.

## Our consciousness is the bridge between dimensions.

By learning how to direct our attention, we can learn to be in tune with every (energetic) part of us: the physical, the emotional, and the spiritual. An old soul, then, has the potential to access invaluable information, tools, skills, and life experience that can support and serve them as life unfolds.

# Soul Mates

Most people have the desire to feel deeply loved, heard, and understood by another human being. The idea that there is someone out there who almost inherently feels that way about us is a source of inspiration, hope, and strength for many. It feeds the countless love stories and fairy tales about love at first sight and the "happily ever after" that seems to effortlessly result from it because the two lovers were simply meant to be together. They were soul mates.

What exactly is a soul mate? The simplest explanation is that a soul mate is someone whose soul is connected to yours.

How did that happen?!

We explored the idea that our souls are each a little piece of the Divine, so we can imagine that every soul is "born" from this Divine. And just like twins share many of the same attributes because they were born from the same parents, at the same moment, in the same place, under the same circumstances, sharing the same DNA, soul mates are those souls that were born from the Divine in the same "universal moment" and thus share all the energetic and vibrational

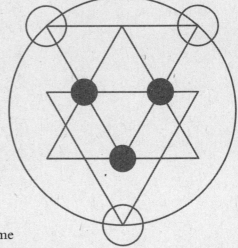

qualities that are connected to that moment. You could say that soul mates have the same vibrational frequency at their essence. This is why they are often instantly attracted to each other. Their vibrations are so similar that they are simply pulled to each other like magnets.

We know that twins are often connected in ways that go beyond what could be explained by their biological sameness. This goes for soul mates as well; they share the spiritual and energetic sameness that connects them in multidimensional ways. Because they share this unique sameness at an energetic core level, they often understand each other effortlessly and pick up on each other's energy over great distances (remember that in multidimensionality there is neither time nor distance). When they meet, they simply "get" each other. Because their connection is so natural, they have tremendous potential for supporting each other's growth and evolution. They mirror and reflect each other in a way that non–soul mates have to work much harder at. This is why soul mates often keep returning to each other throughout many lifetimes, as they can support each other on their life journeys more than anybody.

Some believe we have many soul mates; others believe we have only one. Personally, I feel that the idea of multiple soul mates makes beautiful sense.

I envision how a divine magic wand touches the perfect vibrational moment at Source and sparks the birth of a multitude of new souls, all bursting out from that instant in a cloud of shining and sparkling soul dust. Because they all originate from the same moment, they are in essence the same, carrying similar vibrations that will always be at their cores, no matter what their physical human forms will look like. This soul group is our personal support that shows up in our lives to help us forward on our journeys. It's like our own "family" of earth angels who are here in physical bodies to walk the path with us. Whether we recognize each other when we meet depends on our individual states of consciousness at that time. The more aware we are, the more we are tapped into our magical powers, the easier it will be to recognize the divine vibrational sameness in someone else.

We are living longer than humans ever have, so most of us will have several significant relationships at different stages in our lives. In addition, our expanding consciousness is rapidly increasing our understanding of the multidimensional essence of human beings and souls. A multitude of soul mates—either romantic or otherwise— seems not only desirable but logical in the evolutionary journey of a soul in a human body.

## Soul Mates and Love

Not all our soul mates will be romantic partners. Some will be our friends or our family members. And not all of them will be with us our whole lives. Sometimes we need a soul mate to come into our lives at a certain time in order for us to move to the next phase in our lives. Once the transformation is over, they might leave, as their "task" is done. Often, though, soul mates find each other and stay in each other's lives for prolonged periods of time or for a lifetime in the form of a partner, parent, sibling, family member, or friend.

Probably the most desired and idealized soul mate relationship is that of a romantic partner, as we believe that could be our "one true love." When soul mates are romantic partners, the relationship is often deeply loving and connected, a source for ongoing personal transformation and growth. As soul mates have the same vibrational frequency at their cores, the connection is often effortless and gives a sense of "being at home." There is no need to play games or hide anything because our soul mates can see both our light and our dark. This doesn't mean that soul mate relationships are without challenge. On the contrary, more than anybody soul mates can be the mirrors in which we see ourselves reflected; therefore, they contribute to our personal evolution like no other.

# Tune In

Take a deep breath and enter Perceptual Mode. Give yourself permission to let go of your day, your week, your obligations, your responsibilities, and even your name and the personality others know you through.

Sit in this open space that emerges when you let go of all this. Observe what arises. Are there colors? Sounds? Images? A place? A memory? A sense of connection? Or is there nothing?

Use whatever emerges in this space as a mirror. What does it tell you about who you are?

Observe your feelings while you are in this space. How do you feel?

When you feel you have understood this space, bring your awareness back to your body and the physical world.

In your journal you might record what it felt like to let go and be in open space and note what you understood about yourself as a soul as you sat there.

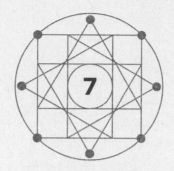

# PURPOSE:
# THE POWER OF VISION

*A goal is not always meant to be reached.*
*It often serves simply as something to aim at.*

**BRUCE LEE, ACTOR**

We now have a more expanded idea of our reality and who we are. Not only did we learn that the world we thought was physical is in fact all energy and vibration, but we even discovered that we are much more than just our physical bodies. We are multidimensional vibrational beings who are deeply connected, entangled, and in co-creation with something much larger, the Divine or Creative Source. We each carry a little piece of this Source inside us that is uniquely ours yet part of that Divine at the same time: our souls. Our magic comes from our entanglement with that Creative Source. Quantum physics offers a useful analogy for understanding the depth of our connection with Source. Quantum *entanglement* refers to a pair or group of subatomic particles interacting with one another in such a way that no individual particle can be described independently of the  others. It's a dance of deep interdependence. It makes entanglement more than a simple connection, as there is an element of merging and interaction associated with it. When we are entangled with Source, we are no longer separate from Source, nor is Source separate from us. And the stronger the connection between you and this Creative Source, the more powerful you are in your ability to create and perform your magic.

## Live, Love, Matter

We are the only species on earth that is inquisitive about our reason for being here, on earth, in a body, alive. We seek meaning and purpose, a connection to the whole, our place in the universe. Almost all human beings have some sort of higher power they worship, look to for guidance, and make the center of their lives. Almost everybody, regardless of culture and religion, believes in a soul that is eternal and infinite, whether it expresses itself through multiple incarnations or as a single self that moves on to an eternal life.

Just like the universe is always moving, morphing, expanding, contracting, pushing, and pulling, so is everything in nature constantly changing and transitioning from one state to the next. There is simply no such thing as a motionless status quo. Life is about change and movement, death and rebirth. What sets humans apart from the rest of all species that follow these same cycles is our consciousness. This consciousness gives rise to self-awareness, and self-awareness inspires personal growth and development. We are not just concerned with survival on a physical level (procreation, food, safety); we want to improve ourselves and our world. We have an innate drive to push forward and to make the next moment "better" or larger than this one. We want to take advantage of the fact that there is not an unchanging status quo; we want to deliberately make *ourselves* better than we were before. Most of us want a higher purpose in our lives, the feeling that we contribute to the whole, the awareness of personal growth and evolution. We dream of our futures, the things we want to create. We set goals; we push ourselves to do better, be better, make a difference, leave a mark.

Life is more than just surviving every day. We want to *live*. We want to *love*. And we want to *matter*.

Our fulfillment comes from
our accomplishments,
our contributions,
and our growth.

# The School of Life

In the last chapter we explored the concept that although our physical bodies are mortal, we each have a larger part that is infinite and eternal, our souls. We also explored the idea that the soul binds our lifetimes here on earth together. We continue to be reborn as the same soul, yet in different physical bodies. The more we return this way, the more experienced we become in "being human." Old souls are those who have lived many lifetimes. You have to wonder, though: What is it that keeps us wanting to come back and continue our journey? There must be something that is so exciting and fulfilling we can't wait to return and do it all over again. We're here with a spiritual desire to learn.

What if all this—meaning earth—is like a school of life? An opportunity for a soul to experience what it is like to live as an energetic consciousness in a corporeal form—a physical body—and be in relationship and co-creation with others as well as with the Divine.

We can then imagine that a lifetime as a soul in a human body is full of new experiences, mysteries, and wonderment. There is so much to learn and discover, and everything is new and exciting. Whether or not we believe in reincarnation, whether we've arrived on earth for the first and only time or for another lifetime's experience, the remembrance of our origin in the Divine and, if our belief system includes past lives, our experiences of the last time are stored somewhere in the layers of our energetic beings, our souls. How much we can access the treasures of information, experience, tools, and skills that are stored in these layers depends on our level of consciousness. And in a beautiful multidimensional way, the opposite is true as well: our level of consciousness depends on how much we can access the experience, tools, and skills that are stored in the subtle (soul) layers of our beings.

Life is all about exploring, discovering, and learning through relationships and experiences that help us grow and evolve. And the more we do it, the better we get. Just like in school, where in each grade our level of skill and knowledge expands and lifts us to the next level. The same goes for souls; with each lifetime we strengthen our remembrance of our origin in the Divine, and the level of experience expands and lifts us to the next level of awareness. Unlike "normal" schools, the school of life never ends. When our corporeal bodies die at the end of our lives and we transition to another state of being, we can return in a new physical form, with the richness of all our previous lives' experiences stored in our beings, if our belief systems make this an available reality for us. If our belief systems do not include reincarnation, we understand our transition to be a transcendent return to the spiritual domain from which we emerged, where we are in a nearer and more immediate relationship to the Divine that gifted us with our human lives.

## The more we awaken our abilities to access the subtle layers, the more awake we will become.

My understanding is that we reincarnate through several cycles to continue our evolution as spiritual beings, and those whose belief system does not include reincarnation do not seek to remember past incarnations. Remembering past lives requires focused awareness, so those who do not seek them will not remember them, though they may have access to information and skills acquired in past lives if their intuition allows it. The cycle of life is thus not a circle but a spiral—even for those who do not have a conscious awareness of reincarnation—where each time we come back or transition we start at the next level. Our maturity is determined by our life experience, and many life experiences make for an old soul—whether those life experiences are accumulated over many human lives or in a unique human lifetime. Because some souls are choosing human incarnation for the first time while others are choosing to return after multiple human incarnations, younger souls interact with old souls who have acquired their depth from many turns of the spiral.

The model of the school of life is based on an interlayered, multi-dimensional relationship and co-creation between souls, humans, planet earth, and the Divine. And the sole purpose of the school is to learn how to make them all work together in harmony. As everything is energy, everything is connected and interrelated. We all contribute to the unfolding of our own lives as much as we contribute to the lives of others and to the whole. The butterfly effect reminds us that something as small as a butterfly flapping its wings can begin a series of events that influence a tornado on the other side of the world. Similarly, our ways of being and doing have an effect on the whole. This means that what you do with your life has an impact on the world. That is the magic of life, and it is at the very foundation of the magic of you.

## What Do You Want to Be When You Grow Up?

From an early age we ask ourselves and each other what we want to do with our lives. While the answer is certainly culturally driven—meaning that our backgrounds have a big influence on the direction we are inspired to take our lives—the drive to reach a goal and make a difference might be more than that. For instance, if your father is a firefighter, and his father was a firefighter, the likelihood of becoming a firefighter yourself is far higher than for someone who doesn't have that family history. If both your parents attended college, you are more likely to attend college as well. And the other way around: when neither of your parents attended college, it becomes a far less likely "automatic" option for you. The accomplishments of our parents and the aspirations they have for us are a big influence on the options that we even *consider* for ourselves. Yet our childhood dreams for what we want to become are often based on our heroes and our desire to save the world, rescue the damsel in distress, make things better, and leave a mark. We seem to have an innate drive to improve ourselves and contribute to the collective at the same time. We want to make a difference.

## Our vision is paramount to our ability to create a reality that we desire.

Some people know exactly what they want to be or the things they want to accomplish. They want to be lawyers, schoolteachers, or professional football players. They might have a clearly defined physical goal for their life, like "living in a big white house in Hawaii" or

"having 10 million dollars in the bank," or it could be a more conceptual and spiritual destination like "living a meaningful life that is based around a deep and thriving love relationship" or "creating a world free of cancer."

Right now, take a few moments to contemplate what it is that you want to accomplish. Have you ever thought about it? Do you have a specific goal? Do you know in what direction you want to steer your life? What is your vision?

Perhaps you don't have a clear vision or goal for your life (yet), but you probably already work with vision and intention on a smaller scale every day. You set an intention, a goal, a destination, even just for that day. This could be that you want to mow the lawn, clean the fridge, call your mother, pay a bill, finish that project, spend time with your children, or go to the gym. Most of us set many small goals for ourselves constantly so that we keep moving through our days with a feeling of accomplishment. We create daily, weekly, monthly, yearly, and life goals this way. It is our way to keep moving forward and expand ourselves and our lives to the next level. By setting an intention and stating clearly *what* we want to accomplish and by when, it is much easier to focus our actions toward that goal. It is also much easier for the Universe to support you in your goals when you are clear and intentional.

# The Magic of Vision

We saw in chapter 2 (Magic: The Power of Belief) how important it is for a magician to be unwavering in their conviction and their vision of what they want to create. To be a powerful sorcerer who can alter their existing reality into one they desire, there can be no doubt, no distraction, and nothing to divert the magician's focus and energy from their magic. The more focused your attention the more powerful your magic.

In the same way, your vision—whether big or small, short or long term—is going to determine where you focus your attention, and where you focus your attention is where you direct your energy, and where you direct your energy is what you create more of. This is the Law of Attraction, which states that "like attracts like." Remember how we discovered that your attention can change the way energy behaves? The field of unlimited potential cannot respond any other way than to align itself to whatever strong and focused energy you send into it. You are responsible for aligning with the field, since the field is what it is: an unlimited and dynamic source of possibilities. The clearer you are about your vision or goal, the easier it will be to align your reality to enlist support from it. When you fully embody your vision and communicate and express it with clarity and in perfect alignment with what you believe to be true, possibilities become infinite.

In multidimensional awareness, we recognize that there are multiple paths to any one place. In other words, there is always more than one way to reach an outcome.

If your goal is to live in a big white house in Hawaii, there are numerous ways it could happen. Working for it is one—and even within that option there are many possibilities—or perhaps you could inherit it, win it, build it, or marry someone who already has it. The point is that it is more important to be clear about the desired outcome (the *what*) than the exact actions to take to get there (the *how*). The field of unlimited potential holds within it exactly that: unlimited potential that we have no ability to completely comprehend or grasp. Our role is to clarify our vision and strengthen our perception in order to recognize and act on the possibilities it generates. Perceptual Mode is the most powerful tool you have for realizing the life you envision.

Your task is to be as intentional as possible in focusing your energy on the outcome. The field will provide the means to get there. Often the result will unfold in ways that you couldn't even have imagined. This is the true magic of living in a multidimensional universe: we affect our reality through our consciousness—our intention and energy—even though the path to get there might be hidden, unknown, mysterious, and unexpected. It might even change while we move along it.

Our main task is to maintain our awareness so we can perceive the path opening before us. For that we need to shift into Perceptual Mode so that we can recognize the possibilities that are presented to us at every moment. Sometimes what seems to be an obstacle on a journey is the path itself. The destination,

too, may change as we grow. A specific, concrete destination can inspire us to set out, but the compass for our journey is the energy we want to create or experience in our lives. In our earlier example of the vision to live in a big white house in Hawaii, we might set out with the intention to achieve just that—the big white house in Hawaii—yet we may discover along the way that what we really desired was a feeling of being at home in a place that inspires and comforts us.

The personal vision I defined a while ago is as follows: to collaborate with other powerful, conscious, and loving leaders to support transformation, awareness, and kindness in a world awakening to a multidimensional reality.

Notice that this is more about a flavor of experience and energy I want to have than about a specific destination or material goal. It is also about my desire to contribute. My higher purpose is that I am here to bridge the world of Spirit and the world of matter. I am a conduit, a storyteller... and my language goes beyond words. I am an illuminator, here to bring that which is hidden in the dark, mysterious and unknown, into the light, so it can be seen and understood.

## Be a Vibrational Match to Your Desires

To move your life in the direction of your vision, you need to recognize when your vision is authentic to your purpose. You also need to shift into Perceptual Mode to perceive the possibilities that are opening around you and align your vibrational expression with your vision.

By being a vibrational match to what you want to create or have, you vibrate with a clear intention and vision. You are then better able to align with the Universe and perceive what it can express, given its unlimited creativity and potential. You will recognize circumstances and people as opportunities, catalysts, and co-creators that will enable you to realize your vision. If you are unclear about your dreams or doubt that the Universe is a willing collaborator, you will fall out of alignment or set up a vibration that doesn't fully support you. This doesn't cancel your progress thus far; it just extends your path to your dream, which may be exactly what's necessary for your growth. This is about a process (a journey)—that's the primary energy. The outcome—the manifestation of that energy—is secondary. Focus on enjoying the process and being alert to what it offers, and you'll arrive at your goal in a form that's appropriate to your truest intentions.

This means that you have to be mindful of your words, your thoughts, and your intentions. Ask yourself if your mind frame and actions are aligned with the vision you have for your future.

I know that most of us were taught to not daydream so much and stay with what is going on in the "real world." I am suggesting that in a complementary framework, daydreaming balances the kind of logistical thinking that people meant when they said "pay attention." Daydreaming—another word for visualization—is a powerful tool to let the Universe know what you desire. Being really clear in what you want—seeing it, hearing it, tasting it, and touching it in your imagination—is the way to manifest it. When you imagine experiencing it even before it manifests, you are communicating to the Universe that this is what you want. If you can dream it, you can create it. Your job is to hold the vibration of your dream and allow the Universe to wrap a reality around you that is aligned with that dream.

# Tune In

Follow your breath into Perceptual Mode and think of a moment or time in your life when you were incredibly lit up, fulfilled, happy. Everything was going well, and you didn't think that life could get any better. Perhaps it was the best day of your life, or the most amazing moment you ever had.

Where are you? Who are you with? What are you doing? What makes it so incredibly fantastic? How do you feel?

Stay in this feeling for a few moments, really taking it in and noticing all the details. Can you be in this moment rather than just remembering it?

Now focus on clarifying your sense of the quality of this feeling. Is it a quality of contributing? Creating? Discovering? Collaborating? Nurturing? Generating wealth?

How can you express this quality in your life? Expressing this quality and the feelings that are related to it is your higher purpose or vision.

Journal about these qualities and imagine specific ways you express them in your life. What are you here to do or share with the world? This could be as grand as writing a bestselling novel or as impactful as practicing absolute inner peace and compassion in every moment.

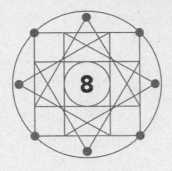

# THE GAP:
# THE POWER OF AWARENESS

*The key to growth is the introduction of higher dimensions of consciousness into our awareness.*

**SUFI PIR VILAYAT INAYAT KHAN, SPIRITUAL MASTER**

We discovered that vision and purpose are powerful driving forces behind our growth and evolution. Without them it would be hard to take our lives in any particular direction. Without direction we would easily fall into a life of repetition and status quo, not of magic and co-creation. We could then lose sight of exciting new discoveries that nourish our growth and expand our consciousness, thus losing our ability to create lives that we are truly excited about. By holding a vision and setting goals—smaller and larger ones—we ensure an ongoing momentum toward becoming more than we were before.

Now that we understand how important it is to have a vision or goal, let's look at how to arrive at a clear vision and figure out what stands between you and making that vision come true. What is creating the gap?

## Integrative Vision

While some people already have a clear vision of what they want to accomplish, you might only have a vague idea of what direction you want to go in, or your vision may not be an integrated one. What I mean by that is that your vision or goal might be very specific and only be about one aspect of your life. It is important to include all the different areas of your life in your vision so it becomes an "integrative vision." The more your vision includes every aspect of your life, the more powerful your magic and ability to create will be. Greater integration generates a clearer vibration. You cannot fully hold a high vibration of a vision for something amazing if your lifestyle is not aligned with or is even completely opposite to that vision. This means that you have to integrate areas like work, career, health, relationships, wealth, hobbies, and your contribution to the whole into your vision as well.

Let's stay with our example goal of "living in a big white house in Hawaii." This vision should include more than just the physical house. Ask yourself questions like these: Who are you with in that house? What does your life there look like? What do you spend your days doing in that house? How do you feel? Are you happy? If so, what exactly makes you so happy? It is probably not *just* the fact that you live in a big white house in Hawaii . . .

You can fully create, visualize, and daydream your desired life like this. The more detailed and complete your vision, including every little aspect of your life, the more coherent your energy will be. Think back to chapter 5 (Energy: The Power of Consciousness) and how we discovered that you have an energy field around you that is the sum of you, your body, your words, your thoughts, and your feelings. When everything about you is aligned with your vision of your life as a whole, your overall energy reflects that. When you say, think, do, feel, intend, express, and envision yourself a certain way, then you *become* that. It will be who you *are*. You embody your vision.

Your body and mind
together determine your
state of being.

The most powerful thing you can do as a co-creator of your life is to focus on your vision and especially the feelings, emotions, words, and thoughts around it, since those make up the essence of your energy field. Greater coherence at every level of your energy— emotional, cognitive, spiritual—generates a stronger, more complex, and more nuanced essence. That is the signal you broadcast into the

Universe with your wish list. It is the *what* of your vision. The stronger your signal, the clearer the Universe will receive it and respond. Your mind generates your thoughts; your mind and body generate your feelings and emotions. So, to make your energy field one coherent bubble that broadcasts exactly what you desire, you need your body and mind to be on the same wavelength.

If your dream is to lie by the pool of your big white house in Hawaii, visualize who you are lying with, what you are doing, the music you are listening to, what the weather is like, the colors of the sky and the water, the sounds in the air, what you are smelling, how you are feeling, how your body is feeling, and how you are going to spend your time afterward. Make your dream so complete, detailed, exciting, and amazing that you can literally *feel* and *see* yourself there. Let your vision generate and amplify your feelings about your goals for your future. That is when your whole being will be tuned in to your vision and everything about you will transmit and vibrate that signal out. Your mind (thoughts) and body (feelings) are humming at the same frequency. The Universe cannot do anything else but arrange itself according to the energetic essence of your signal (your vision) as you perceive it, so you'll attract people and circumstances that vibrate in complementary frequencies. In that manner you, the field, and those whose visions align with yours will create a reality that is an expression of your energy and supports you in realizing your vision.

## Yes, but How?

Although there are practical steps you can take to bring you closer to achieving your vision, you don't need to know all the details of *how* to get to your goal. For instance, if your dream is to become a cardiovascular surgeon, then, of course, you set yourself up for success by following an educational path that will provide you with the required knowledge and certifications. Yet how this is all going to unfold in a complete life around your dream of being a surgeon entails many other details that we are leaving to the Universe. Remember that the way you communicate with the Universe is through your thoughts and feelings. So, the more you fully embody your dream of being a surgeon—through your thoughts and your feelings—the stronger your "surgeon" signal to the Universe will be. The quantum field can align you with circumstances and people that support your vision. Exactly *how* that is all going to happen is not for you to figure out. That is not your task to know nor organize. All you need to do is stay aware of all the subtle details so you don't miss any of the opportunities the Universe places along your path. You can daydream or visualize in great detail what a day as a surgeon would look like. Where do you live? Are you living alone, or do you have a partner? Where is your home? What does it look like? Feel like? What is your routine when you get up and get ready for a day at work? What does it feel like when you are in the operating room? What makes your work so fulfilling?

Focus on the *what* and leave the *how* to the Universe.

# That's Not What I Want!

Do you recognize this? You are not really sure yet what your vision is or where you want to take your life. You don't have a set goal, and you are okay with that for the time being. Unfortunately, you keep finding yourself in situations and with people you don't like at all. You wonder how that keeps happening to you. Although you are not sure what it is you *do* want, this certainly isn't it.

Often, to arrive at what we do want in our lives, we have to figure out what we don't want so that we learn the difference. This way, we become aware of the dynamics of the elements that create our reality. Only when we recognize our own contributions to the circumstances and people showing up in our lives, both positive and negative, can we be conscious creators of our own lives.

Have you ever noticed how much time and energy we put toward all the things we *don't* want? We seem to have more to say about everything that we don't like than the things we do, whether it is the weather, politics, our bodies, our partners, our health, our neighbors, our in-laws, our bosses, the economy, what's on TV, celebrities, or the latest trend. Even our news coverage focuses more on the things that are "wrong" and "bad" with the world than all the wonderful and uplifting things that are happening. Because the good stuff *is* happening as well, but collectively we pay more attention to the negatives than the positives.

It is unlikely that we can create the positive world we want by putting all our attention, and thus our energy, toward the negative. When all you see and hear around you is bad news and sad stories, it is very hard to maintain a positive attitude—meaning generating and maintaining happy thoughts, feelings, and emotions. And guess what you'll attract more of when you walk around with a negative outlook?

## The Law of Attraction

Since your thoughts, your feelings, your words, and your intentions all together create your specific energy frequency, you attract circumstances and people into your life that match that frequency. So, when you walk around with a dark cloud hanging over your head, it is very likely that you will attract circumstances and people that align with your dark cloud. The saying "misery likes company" is a great reflection of how this works. When you don't feel great, you don't want to be around people who are happy, chipper, and upbeat, as that will make you more aware of the contrast between them and you. And they don't want to be around you, either. So, you look for or unconsciously attract others who feel the same as you do, because you carry the same vibration. Your energy fields have a similar flavor. They feel like kindred spirits, and that makes you feel like you connect or belong.

Of course, this works the other way around as well: when you feel great, happy, excited, inspired, and uplifted, you attract others who feel that way as well. They recognize the flavor of your energy field even beyond your obvious body language.

As the Law of Attraction states, "like attracts like." Our thoughts and feelings are all made of energy, and we attract people and circumstances in our lives that are a vibrational match with those thoughts and feelings.

## Pay Attention!

We are so used to living in a 3D world focused on all things physical and linear that we easily miss the subtle signs and opportunities that emerge around us. We often don't even consider all the channels that are open to us in support of reaching our goals. The paradigm we grew up with did not include the belief that we have magic at our core and that we are in constant co-creation with the Divine. And it certainly did not teach us *how* to use our magic and manifestation power. We have been living in a world based on 3D laws about physical causes and reactions. We don't realize that we can cause reactions ourselves with our thoughts, words, and feelings.

When the quantum field starts organizing itself around the signal you are sending out, it often expresses very subtle things first. Like the example in chapter 5 about sending out a "red" thought and noticing "red" occurrences around you. Because of the subtle nature of these reactions to your signal, they often seem only indirectly related to your vision . . . so you don't always notice. You don't recognize them as the Universe's answer to your vision or prayer, as you are looking for the "big" delivery. You do not expect to get to your goal in many subtle, often unpredictable, small steps. Yet, this is how the magic of co-creation with the Universe really works. It's all one big "soup" of energy—a field of unlimited potential, aka the quantum field—that organizes itself in cycles, patterns, rhythms, and structures under the influence of the energy that *you* launch into it.

The subtle stuff that the Universe aligns you with could include someone you make a connection with at an event seemingly unrelated to your vision. Because they have nothing to do with your goal you might not recognize the significance of their appearance on your path, but they might turn out to be essential in an introduction to someone else who *does* have to do with your vision. Or it might be that you feel a sudden urge to go to the beach, even though that was not in your plan for the day. Perhaps, when you get to the beach, you run into the best thing that ever happened to you, which will eventually lead you to your vision.

# What we think, where we focus our attention, what we expect, what we believe, and what we say out loud... all of it matters (as in, can *become matter*, become "real").

You see, the Universe is much larger than what you and I can see from our limited points of view. Everything is connected, including all the stuff that is outside our direct experience and reality. Your focused attention—your signal—starts pulling things, people, and circumstances to you that have the same vibration as your signal. Perhaps it's only one small, subtle thing at first, but then, when you become aware of it, you start looking for other signs and synchronicities that align with your vision. The more you do this, the more you focus your attention and thus direct your energy to your vision. You might start believing that it can happen and expecting it to manifest. You might tell your friends how these things are showing up "all of a sudden." All this has an accelerating effect on what you are attracting.

# Tune In

To attract what we really desire, we have to be aware of what we are attracting *right now* and how we are contributing to that. For this exercise, we are going to focus on one specific area of attraction: people who are *not* aligned with what we desire. They might be triggering us, bringing up negative feelings or thoughts. They might be blocking us from living in our happy place by making it difficult to maintain our awareness when we are interacting with them. Since we are all mirrors for each other, these triggers show us something about ourselves. We can teach ourselves *about* ourselves by using these people as mirrors.

▲ Close your eyes if that feels good to you. Follow your breath into Perceptual Mode. Focus on one specific person who triggers you or brings up undesired feelings. Be with them for a moment.

▲ What don't you like about them? How did this person come into your life? What is it that triggers you about them? How do you feel when that happens?

▲ What impression of yourself do you get when you see yourself reflected in the mirror that this person offers you? For example, perhaps you feel this person is judgmental. How does that reflect on you? Are you perhaps judgmental toward yourself? Are you being judgmental toward yourself for being judgmental toward others? Pay attention to the specifics of what you feel this person judges you for and what you are judging others for.

▲ Once you have identified what you are judging yourself or others for, bring your awareness to that quality. For example, you might have a sense of scarcity, competitiveness, or being too positive.

▲ Resting in Perceptual Mode, allow that quality to acquire a texture, a feeling, a sound, or an image. Pay attention to your body, any place you feel tightness or a blockage. Allow your sense of this quality into your awareness and simply observe it until you feel it starts moving and changing.

▲ Allow it to continue moving, changing, and dissolving until you have open space or a sense of flow. While you are in Perceptual Mode, this will happen automatically when you bring your attention and awareness to whatever is blocking your path and your growth.

▲ Bring the person you started with back into your awareness and notice how you feel now. Did your feeling change?

▲ When we're dealing with people we've had long and complicated relationships with, we might find we have to do this process several times for energy to move.

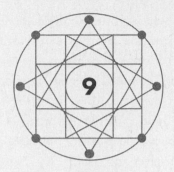

# STORIES:
# THE POWER OF THOUGHTS
# AND WORDS

*I meant what I said and I said what I meant.*

DR. SEUSS, AUTHOR

We saw that what stands between you and your ability to co-create your dream or vision with the Universe is your awareness. We discovered that your thoughts, words, feelings, and intentions are paramount to your magical powers, and your vision has to be integrated in all aspects of your life to have an optimal effect. We also looked at how the Universe works and how important it is to pay attention to every little detail so you don't miss any opportunity to get closer to your vision or your dream.

Who and what shows up in your life depends on your awareness of the thoughts you think, the feelings you feel, the words you use, and the relationship between all of them.

We are now going to look closer at the stories we tell. As the constructs that direct our lives, they lie at the core of our magical abilities. Often our limiting beliefs (which are in the way of our magical power) are buried deep inside ourselves and will surface in the stories we tell ourselves and others. By changing our stories, we can change our lives.

## The Biggest Story of All

Storytelling has been around as long as humans have existed. Stories offer a powerful way to record history, convey messages, motivate, teach, help us understand ourselves, and, ultimately, transform us. Concepts that are hard to explain in a linear fashion are often easier to understand when offered in a metaphor or tale. You've probably noticed that much of the information that comes to you in Perceptual Mode arrives in the form of images, metaphors, or stories—not arguments or theoretical constructs.

Perhaps the biggest story of all is the one we tell about who we are as human beings and why we are here on earth. It is a story that has been told since the beginning of time, throughout all cultures, on all continents, in many different languages, and in many different forms. Sometimes this story is one of inclusion, showing an understanding of a bigger picture in which humans are deeply connected to the planet and a divine Source. Other times the story tells the tale of a human who is completely separate from the Divine. Regardless of the stories told, they all derive from an intrinsic desire to explain our existence and reason for being here. This "big story" changes and evolves—just like we do—in alignment with our collective consciousness, which is expanding thanks to ongoing scientific discovery, deeper spiritual understanding, and social and cultural changes.

The "big story" you grow up with forms the basis of how you see yourself, how you see the world, and how you see the possibility of co-creation with something larger than you.

## Stories Hold Energy

Stories are containers for energy. They can bridge the world of energy and the world of form and manifestation. Whether written in words, animated in movies, or visualized in art, stories not only describe a series of events but also affect the way we feel and the way we think. Love stories, for instance, can make us feel hopeful that true connection is possible and motivate us to keep our hearts open. Scary stories can make us aware of the darker aspects of life and inspire us to pay attention and work on our skills to handle life's opposites. Stories about real people who did something amazing can motivate us to give direction to our lives.

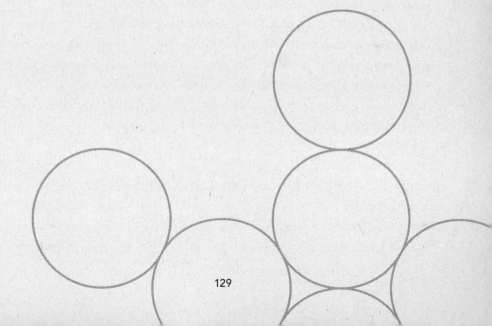

We watch movies and read
books because we seek
to be distracted, uplifted,
motivated, educated,
excited, or inspired.

We all know how much a movie or a book can change our moods, yet we often don't realize that the stories we tell ourselves do the same—they create a container of energy as well. We tell stories about our lives, our world, others, and especially ourselves, and they all become part of our personal energy bubble. When I talk about "the stories you tell," I don't only mean the ones you say out loud. I am also referring to the ones that may be running in your head without you being aware of them, stories you don't share with others or even with yourself on a conscious level. Even if you don't say them out loud, their energy "colors" your personal energy field and tunes the signal that you are sending the Universe.

## What Stories Do You Tell?

We all tell stories about who we are, where we are from, what happened to us, and where we are going. We like some of the things we tell stories about, but a lot of them we don't like or we want to change. Because we find it difficult to accept that we have partici-pated in creating what we don't like about our lives, we sometimes unconsciously hang on to stories that, ironically, keep us stuck in the very place or situation we want to escape. They limit us to an expres-sion of ourselves that feels too small or somehow "out of alignment" with our true selves.

Often our stories are about what others have done *to* us rather than about how *we* have made choices and constructed a reality. We choose, consciously or not, how to *respond* to the people and situa-tions in our lives.

Sometimes the stories we tell (ourselves) about our early life expe-riences will make up the majority of our stories for the rest of our lives. They reflect the extent to which we have processed and inte-grated our experiences. If you had a bad experience when you were six years old and you have not been able to move on from it, it will be reflected in the stories you tell yourself and others about yourself. The experience can still feel very real to you today because it is made real again whenever you retell it. Whether you say it out loud to tell others who you are or use it to remind yourself of who you believe you are, it sits at the core of your attention and even primes you to repeat that experience. It will continue to do so until you have the opportunity to resolve the challenge or heal the trauma.

Often, we hold on to these experiences tightly and identify ourselves accordingly simply because we don't have the maturity, wis-dom, and awareness to process and integrate them with the awareness that we are active co-creators of our lives. Because your thoughts and stories still revolve around your bad experience, you keep attracting people and circumstances into your life that are aligned with it, and so you keep the experience alive.

The stories you tell broadcast a signal into the Universe. Even when you have a dream or vision of something that you would like to accomplish, if most of what you do, say, think, and feel is still about your bad experience, the signal you send out into the quantum field is really not about your vision but instead about your bad experience . . . and so you keep creating more of it. Remember that to send a coherent "wish list" to the Universe, your mind and body need to tell the same story; your thoughts and your feelings need to align. It is not enough to think hopeful happy thoughts while you feel miserable or while you tell yourself stories of misery, hopelessness, or suppression. That's why affirmations by themselves are not enough. Unless they are aligned with your feelings, they are not going to be effective.

# Your thoughts and feelings together are your vibrational point of attraction.

This book is all about how you are at the core of everything that goes on in your life; you determine who and what shows up in it. Your magical powers lie in your ability to affect your life with your thoughts, feelings, words, intentions, and actions—through your stories and the ways you live them out. You can rise above the idea that you are "just a victim" as you start to understand the role you play in your circumstances and how you have the power to change your life by changing your perspective. While we cannot always control what is happening, we can control how we respond. Staying in the victim role because something bad happened to us earlier in life is a choice that we make. By no means am I dismissing the sometimes-horrific things that you might have gone through, but you do not have to be what your past trauma has made you; you can redeem your trauma by transforming it into a story of learning, of strength, of your sense of compassion and your commitment to justice. This recognition of your magic, your ability to transform your experience, gives you the power to decide how you want to respond. The story we create around any experience is going to be reflected in what unfolds around us. We can be protagonists—active creators of our stories—rather than victims of stories that we don't author intentionally.

So, what we say, the words we use, and the stories we tell are important, because they are a vibrational point of attraction. Our stories don't just describe our lives, they create our lives. By choosing more consciously, by being aware of the larger context of our experience, we can author stories in which we are never victims and are, instead, the makers of our stories. Using what we learn when we enter into Perceptual Mode, we expand our context to include possibilities we might not otherwise recognize. Instead of seeing obstacles, we see challenges as opportunities for growth. We recognize that challenge is the complement to achievement, that confusion is the complement to discovery. By changing the stories we tell, we can change the energy that supports them and therefore the energy that draws people and circumstances into our lives. By becoming ultra-conscious of every word we say, and even think, we can start understanding and changing the patterns we have created that are reflected in our relationships, our circumstances, the things we attract, and the things that repeat themselves in our lives.

So, what is the story you tell about yourself?

## The Mind and Why It Matters

Once we recognize the stories we are *aware* of telling (the ones we hear ourselves telling others), we begin to see that there are also stories we tell ourselves even when we do not have an audience. Then we can develop our awareness of these stories we never say out loud, stories told in the ways we treat ourselves.

I am sure you have heard the term "subconscious." It refers to the part of the mind that is outside of our conscious awareness, where the prefix "sub" means under or below consciousness. So, all the stuff stored in our subconscious is *under* our consciousness, and we are not fully aware of it. Despite this, the things in our subconscious matter (as in, can *become matter*, become real).

What goes on in our subconscious surfaces in the stories we tell and therefore in the energy our stories create.

As a result, what goes on in our subconscious is reflected in what and who we attract into our lives.

Let's take a look at how all this works.

The mind can be described as the brain in action. The brain is the physical organ that, along with the rest of the nervous system, supports the process of mind. Our minds monitor, respond, and use or transform the energy and information we gather. In fact, the latest research in neuroscience and neuropsychology shows that our minds shape and transform our brains. Our thoughts—the way we direct our attention and develop our awareness—literally generate and alter the physical structures in our brains.

Our minds, not our brains, make sense and meaning of our experiences. The mind organizes the information we gather and directs the energy we engage with or generate in our response to others and the world. When we engage the world with awareness, we respond mindfully and creatively to situations: we can choose the thoughts, process the feelings, and clarify the insights that shape us and the world. Our minds generate our realities because they generate our thoughts, emotions, and visions of ourselves and the world.

We are consciously aware of much of what we do and think, but there is even more that we are not aware of at all. When we are not aware of how and where we're focusing our attention, we are not mindful.

It is helpful to divide the mind into three levels depending on the degree of awareness we have: the unconscious, the conscious, and the subconscious.

## The Unconscious Mind

The unconscious mind is in charge of all the things in your body that are functioning all by themselves without your conscious participation: the immune system, the heart, the digestive system, and hormones, for example. All involuntary bodily functions are in the domain of the unconscious mind. Sometimes this is called the autonomic nervous system.

Another function of your unconscious mind is to take in information through the five senses—sight, smell, sound, taste, and touch—and process it enough to determine whether to bring it to the attention of the conscious mind. For example, when you have a gas leak in your home, your *ability* to smell it happens unconsciously, but you become *aware* of the smell because your unconscious mind is pushing the information to your conscious mind so you can take action and save yourself.

## The Conscious Mind

The conscious part of your mind is in charge of many essential things. It is your "waking" mind, and its specialty is logic and linear thinking. It loves to reason, analyze, plan, organize, evaluate, compare, and control. It is involved in all the thoughts and actions that you are aware of, like the reading that you are doing right now, or the yoga you will be doing later. It helps you learn, and it stores your knowledge in a way that keeps it accessible. Although it is tremendously important and useful, it is limited and only makes up about 5 percent of your mind.

## The Abyss of the Subconscious

Which brings us to the biggest and most mysterious part of your mind: the subconscious. How extensive it is seems to differ depending on what source you consult, but the overall consensus is that it takes up over 90 percent of your mind!

The subconscious is where we store and retrieve information. It is the place where we run the programs that allow us to live our lives without having to think about every little thing over and over again. Many of the things we learn with our conscious minds are stored here and become part of our "automatic" behavior. Driving a car is an example of this; when we first learn how to drive, we are very conscious of everything we do. We *think* about how to use the gears, the blinker lights, the gas pedal, and the mirrors. We tell ourselves to focus, stay aware of our surroundings, anticipate, and react. When we become more skillful, many of these behaviors become subconscious, meaning we (can) perform them without consciously thinking about them all the time.

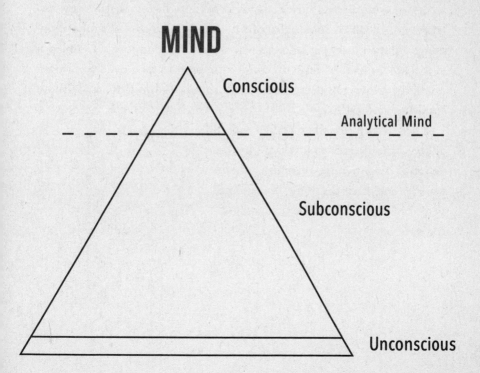

Typing is another skill that we first learn very consciously but then store in our subconscious (and in our muscle memory) so we can run the process automatically, meaning that we don't have to think about it anymore: our fingers automatically know where to go while typing. This is also the case with the way we can automatically punch in phone numbers or PINs without consciously thinking about them. The very opposite might actually happen when we *do* try to consciously think about it: we draw a blank.

This happened to me recently. I arrived at my friend's house for a visit. I had been there many times and had always used the gate code to enter the premises. Since I hadn't been there in a while, I consciously started thinking about the code while I was pulling up to the gate. I got to the little box where I had to punch in the numbers, and I couldn't remember exactly what the code was! I tried a few times with no result. I got a little frustrated because I *knew* that I knew the code . . . at least in some part of my mind. I realized that the more effort I put into trying to recall the numbers, the more scrambled it all became. I had to allow my automatic pilot to take over. So, I took a breath, closed my eyes, cleared my mind, and just did it, without thinking about it . . .

I reached out for the number pad and allowed my fingers to just type in the code. I was literally watching them type! I remember thinking, "Aha! *That* was the number!" while I watched the gate open.

You see, I had performed the action of typing in that particular code so often that it had become a habit. My mind stored the information in my subconscious, and my body stored the pattern of movement that expressed that information. Every time I pulled up to the gate, my subconscious would take over and signal my fingers to repeat the pattern it had stored.

Just as we store actions in our subconscious, we store memories of experiences there as well. Many of these memories we are not consciously aware of anymore, often because they happened a long time ago. They can be brought to our awareness by something in our present that triggers them to surface. For instance, you might encounter the fragrant smell of roses, and all of a sudden you remember how you used to spend time with your grandfather in his rose garden. You had long forgotten this experience; it was stored in your subconscious. The smell triggered your mind to bring it to the surface. This, of course, is a happy memory, and as a result it triggers happy feelings in your present moment. It is almost as if you're reliving your time with your grandfather.

Often, though, the memories triggered by something in the present are of unhappy past experiences, and as a result they generate unhappy feelings. We can find ourselves all of a sudden feeling sad or angry, while we were having a great day. And just as our subconscious drives our car after we've become familiar with a route and a set of behaviors, our subconscious can drive our reactions and emotions.

A remembered feeling that's in motion in our subconscious can shape our reaction in the present and limit our awareness of greater possibility, therefore limiting our ability to create. Anger or sadness stemming from a subconscious memory can drive a reaction that collapses new possibilities into familiar impossibilities. Instead of perceiving the potential that is all around us in the quantum field, we react in ways that express the certainties that arose out of and shaped our past. Our out-of-sync reactions interfere with our ability to perceive the potential that is all around us, trapping us in old stories about ourselves and others. This is how we re-create the very limitations that make us unhappy; *we* define the "reality" that keeps us from experiencing our true potential.

## State of Being

It turns out that by the time we reach our mid-thirties almost everything we do and think is generated from what we stored in our subconscious. Our personality and identity derive from a memorized set of habits, behaviors, emotional responses, beliefs, attitudes, stories, and perceptions that we have stored in our subconscious. These memories are "programmed" into us and now run us. They form the basis of what we think, how we feel, and what we do.

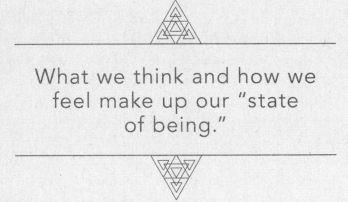

What we think and how we feel make up our "state of being."

From the time we wake up to the time we get home from work, make dinner, watch television, and go to bed, most people's lives are a day-to-day repetition of the same routine and behavior. And therefore, the feelings that are generated are the same day after day as well. When you do the same thing over and over, more than likely you will have the same thoughts and feel the same feelings while doing it. And you will re-create the reality that those thoughts and feelings generate.

We are often not even aware of all our thoughts and feelings that are not aligned with our dream or vision. We may dream of being a big performer on a global stage, yet we walk around feeling unworthy of love, angry about what happened in our past, and in disbelief that anything really great will ever happen to us. We are not a vibrational match to our dreams, and most of what we tell others about ourselves isn't either. When our thoughts and feelings—and thus our state of being—do not align with the visions and goals we have for ourselves, the signals we send to the Universe do not either. So how can we expect the field to organize energy in alignment with our dreams if we ourselves are not in alignment with them? We need to attune ourselves with our dreams and recognize the possibilities the Universe holds out for us so we can align with those possibilities (rather than aligning with the limitations of our old habits, perceptions, and lack of awareness). Then we send the strongest signal we can generate into the field to bring those possibilities to the surface of emergent reality. To optimize our magical ability to co-create with the Universe, our state of being has to match our vision.

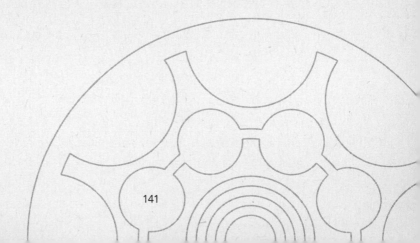

# Beliefs

At the core of most of our stories are the beliefs we have about . . . well, everything: ourselves, others, the world, our jobs, our families, our health, money, politics, celebrities, our neighbors, the weather, God, our partners, love, food, and so on.

A belief is simply a thought that we think over and over again . . . until it becomes a belief. Just like descriptions carry assumptions we don't recognize, our beliefs often carry assumptions we are unaware of. We can create beliefs without even being conscious that we are embedding limitations in those beliefs. Most of our thoughts and beliefs come from our memories and can be discovered in the stories we tell ourselves about the significance or meaning of our experiences. They also arise from our upbringing, going as far back as infancy. This includes culture, schooling, religion, and even the movies, TV shows, books, and songs we were exposed to. Something happened in the past that made us feel a certain way.

## Our beliefs are the foundation of the stories we tell.

Thoughts and emotions are the language of the mind just as physical sensations are the language of the body, so to avoid being blindsided by what's hidden in words, we need to *feel* our way forward. To strengthen and expand our awareness, we need to pay attention to our feelings, both emotional and physical.

We also need to pay attention to the words we use to describe ourselves, others, and the world. Our words carry with them our underlying stories, values, and beliefs. These stories constitute a kind of program that runs in the background, influencing our experiences, shaping our choices, and affecting our ability to create outcomes. Perceptual Mode allows us to feel our way to what's hidden in the stories that are hidden in our words.

Beliefs, in particular, tend to become part of our subconscious, which means that they run in the ongoing program we are not even aware of—laying down its architecture, in a way. This program determines the stories we tell, the words we use, the expectations we have, and the assumptions we make. It directs how we feel and behave. But usually we don't even know we're running this program, or that it is all based on a belief that emerged after an experience we had years or decades ago!

We already saw in chapter 3 (Reality: The Power of Understanding) how our beliefs about the world, about people, and about ourselves shape our perception of reality. These beliefs are mostly hidden in our subconscious and have become part of the programming that now runs our lives. We enact our beliefs in the choices we make, the relationships we create, and the work we find for ourselves. By looking for patterns in these areas, we gain insight into what's hidden in our subconscious program; by shifting into Perceptual Mode, we expand our awareness and deepen our insight.

To change what we attract into our lives, we have to address the underlying beliefs that are determining how we behave, think, and feel. To change the signal that we send out to the Universe and to enlarge our awareness of the possibilities available to us in the quantum field, we have to change our state of being—and for that, we have to find our way into the subconscious so we can rewrite the programs.

# Tune In

Follow your breath into Perceptual Mode and bring into your awareness a belief that you have *about yourself* and that you find clear evidence of in your life.

Focus on patterns as you look for evidence of the beliefs in your hidden programming. Maybe you notice that you keep attracting a certain kind of partner, even though you tell yourself you're not going to make that same "mistake" again, and even though you've done your therapy before choosing your next partner. What is the pattern there? What does that pattern suggest? You might start with a belief statement like "I am not good at romantic relationships," but that's not the whole story. What qualities are hidden in that statement? How would you describe yourself as a person who is "not good" at romantic relationships? Too trusting? Too needy? Too independent? What is the story hidden in the quality you think most determines your experience of romantic relationships?

This same approach will work with any pattern you observe that reveals a belief—for example, a pattern that gives you the belief "I'm not good with money."

Since everything is a reflection of what is going on inside us, there is an insight or lesson there for you, both in the pattern that reveals the belief and in the belief itself.

What is your belief teaching you about how you support yourself and how you limit yourself?

Why do you think you have this belief? Is it based on an experience you had? On something you were taught, or something you read, heard, or observed?

Now, contemplate what this belief causes in your life. How is it holding you back? How is it preventing you from creating what you really desire?

Come up with a statement that starts with "If I didn't believe . . . about myself (or someone else), my life would change . . ."

Take this statement with you while you're in Perceptual Mode and observe what arises in the space that this new statement opens.

Stay with this until you feel that the process is complete.

Now rest your attention on the scenario or the possibility that feels most true to you. Allow that to fill your awareness. When you feel this process is complete, gradually come back to your body and physical reality.

In your journal you might record the blocking belief, then write the new statement, then describe as fully as possible what happened when you took the new statement into Perceptual Mode.

In chapter 12 (Tools: The Power of Doing), I introduce the Modern Merlin Transformation Tool that gives you templates to guide you through the discovery and transformation of hidden beliefs that might be in the way of your magical abilities to create.

Part 3

# YOUR LIFE

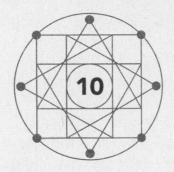

# SACRED GEOMETRY:
# THE POWER OF STRUCTURE

*[The Universe] cannot be read until we have learnt the language
and become familiar with the characters in which it is written.
It is written in mathematical language, and the letters are
triangles, circles and other geometrical figures, without which
means it is humanly impossible to comprehend a single word.*

GALILEO GALILEI, PHYSICIST, PHILOSOPHER, MATHEMATICIAN

I n the last part of this book, we are going to put everything we
have found so far together and integrate it into a workable model
for your life.

Let's start with the model offered by sacred geometry and explore
how it can support you in expanding your awareness of your power

to be a creator of your life experience. Sacred geometry shapes energy into patterns that then can become form. It is a set of rules that form energy and organize templates for matter. By recognizing the shapes, patterns, and repetitions of the natural world around us, we can learn to identify the patterns we use to organize our lives. Sacred geometry helps us become aware of patterns and their influence in our lives: those that are generated by Source and are available to us in the quantum field and those we create through our reactions and responses to our experience.

Creation arises out of (perceived) chaos into harmony according to mathematical principles that describe how Source shapes energy. We can learn to read this universal blueprint, and sacred geometry can help us learn to create harmony in our lives when we perceive them as chaotic. What we often perceive as chaotic can also be understood as the necessary and fertile condition for something new to emerge. What seems destructively chaotic can be an opportunity to create something new if we have tools to help us find patterns in the chaos.

Sacred geometry reminds us that everything in creation is based on the same fundamental principles. At the core, everything is geometric patterns, and these patterns bring harmony to chaos to create a world that expresses aspects of infinite possibility.

Recognizing the patterns within the ebbs and flows of our own lives is at the core of our co-creative power. This is the kind of awareness that allows us to work magic, and this awareness can be called up by going into Perceptual Mode in any situation.

## Blueprint of the Universe

There is so much to discover about sacred geometry. We could go into all the fundamental principles that are at its core, and we could explore it throughout time and history. All this could be—and will be someday—a book by itself, but in *Modern Merlin*, we are going to focus on *how* we can use sacred geometry as a tool to direct our energy (our magic) and choose perceptual modalities.

Throughout history, in countless cultures and on all continents, there have been many indications of our understanding of the relationship between geometric patterns and life itself. We only have to take a closer look at all the structures that are built to honor our gods and goddesses to find that sacred geometry is fundamental to the way we bridge our mundane world and the world of Spirit.

The term "sacred geometry" refers to our understanding that everything in creation is built according to the same rules and geometric proportions, a "divine" (sacred) blueprint underneath it all. Patterns and repetitions of mathematical formulas are the foundation of how things are formed and grow.

## Sacred geometry is at the core of all life.

Think about a sunflower, for instance, how the seeds at the center are formed in beautiful spiral patterns. We find this same spiral principle in many other instances in nature, like vegetables, seashells, star formation, waves, fingerprints, human body proportions, water molecules, and even our DNA. Life continues to create itself according to the same principles. Shapes, patterns, and repetition are the foundation of nature's design. Always. Everywhere. The microcosm is built and formed the same way as the macrocosm. An atom inside your body exists under the same laws as the planets out in the universe. Everything repeats itself.

You could say that sacred geometry is a language. And it is telling the story of creation.

## What Does Sacred Geometry Have to Do with You?

Because sacred geometry is at the core of our beings, we intrinsically feel attracted to sacred geometry designs. Many of our structures, churches, temples, and mosques are built or decorated on the principles of sacred geometry, and even whole cities and landscapes are designed this way.

At the core of sacred geometry are simple symbols and shapes that we all know: circle, square, triangle, cross, and spiral. Many of these symbols are found in the natural world around us. Throughout human history and across cultures we find evidence of the use of shapes and symbology to express our understanding of who we are and how we are connected to everything around us. We often use a mixture of them to express complex concepts and to help us feel that we're part of something larger than we are.

We were using symbols, shapes, and colors to tell stories long before we had words to do so. Often these stories were about creation and how we fit in: stories with many layers, about spiritual beings on a journey in human bodies on a small planet somewhere in an immense galaxy.

Sacred geometry also reminds us that *everything* in life follows patterns and cycles, in both our outer and our inner worlds. By understanding the architectural nature of the Universe, we understand that our lives are constructed the same way and that the ongoing patterns are how life expresses itself. A large part of our development as humans is based on the recognition of these patterns. They help us make sense of the world around us. They are the building blocks of our consciousness. By simply focusing on recognizing these patterns in our experiences, we can reinforce our awareness of our potential to align with these principles and work harmonious magic. We can more readily recognize where our limiting beliefs distort these patterns, and we can focus our awareness on dismantling old patterns and beliefs and generating new ones that bring us into alignment with the creative power of this geometry.

One of the first things babies learn is to recognize shapes and patterns. They are especially drawn to face patterns. Have you ever experienced how babies light up when they recognize a familiar person? They can also recognize sound patterns from a very early stage—even when they are still inside the womb—as they respond to voices or soothing music. All this forms the first steps toward "making sense of the world" and the development of consciousness. When we grow older, our perception of ourselves and our reality continues to build through our evolving relationship with patterns in our environment, our language, and our thoughts. We often organize ourselves socially, culturally, and spiritually based on similarity in perception, behavior, and expression. We often seek out those who seem to be the same as we are and who share similar views, morals, and values. Like attracts like.

Wait . . . doesn't that sound familiar?

Just like our energy attracts people and circumstances who are a vibrational match with ours, we *consciously* seek social, cultural, and spiritual connection with people and circumstances who are aligned with us.

Both our internal and our external worlds are made of patterns and repetitions.

## Why Now?

We see a rising interest in sacred geometry lately. Why?

Our world is changing, and fast. Collectively we are waking up to the understanding that everything is interconnected. That the actions of one person affect all of us, including our earth. The pandemic of 2020 was a powerful example of this; 3D reality showed us how interdependent and interconnected we are on the physical level. What we do and say makes a difference. We are increasingly realizing that living in harmonious co-creation with each other and our earth is the key to true peace and fulfillment.

Sacred geometry can help us connect to our true selves. By recognizing the shapes, patterns, and repetitions of the natural world around us, we can learn to identify the patterns in our lives. When we understand that creation itself is based on these patterns and repetitions, we understand that our lives unfold the same way. So, if we want to change our lives or what is happening in them, we have to look for the patterns and repetitions that created the current situation. Do you find yourself in the same circumstances again and again? Are the people who show up in your life bringing new insights that help you evolve, or are you reliving the same thing but with a different person? Is your life taking you on a spiral path that opens out into new experiences and growth while also bringing you inward to a stronger sense of your connection to Source? This double spiral (a sort of double helix, one could say) is the shape of a creative life moving toward its fullest expression. Moving in a straight line—denying many possibilities or paths in order to defend only one possibility, no matter how limiting or isolating or painful—clearly shows that you are out of alignment with the quantum field of infinite possibility and the sacred geometry that shapes it.

Sacred geometry reminds us that everything in creation is based on the same fundamental principles. At the core, everything is geometric patterns, and these patterns bring harmony to chaos. This applies to both our outer *and* our inner worlds.

Recognizing the patterns
within the ebbs and flows
of our own lives is at the
core of our co-creative and
magical power.

Sacred geometry is a tool to enhance the harmony in our lives. We can use it to create human environments that align with the principles of life. We can surround ourselves with art and design that reflect how life evolves, and we can even decorate our bodies with these sacred symbols. These symbols invite us to hold an intention or belief they represent, and the symbols themselves hold energy. For example, in Reiki, practitioners use symbols to activate energy. We can use these symbols to create more harmony in our lives, to remember who we really are, and to remind ourselves that all life is interconnected.

Sacred geometry designs can awaken and deepen our awareness of the sacred architecture that is at the core of everything.

## Flower of Life

The most well-known sacred geometric design is the Flower of Life. It has been around for centuries, but it has been appearing with greater frequency and resonating with more people over the last few years. Perhaps you have seen it somewhere—in art, in jewelry, and increasingly more in tattoos? The image is acting as a catalyst for more people than ever before because so many people have access to the internet, which allows for the distribution of images across cultures, countries, and continents as well as across different educational and economic levels. This is part of the evolutionary change happening within the human species as people open to their intuitions and to a "feeling" experience of reality instead of a "thinking" experience. This is the shift from 3D into multidimensionality.

The Flower of Life is formed by intersecting circles. This design symbolizes our understanding that everything is connected and that we are all part of a much larger whole. Its basic design element is a circle to remind us that each of us, each component of a living system, is whole and complete.

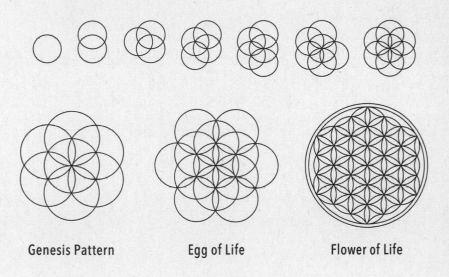

Genesis Pattern        Egg of Life        Flower of Life

The process of creating the Flower of Life from one circle to its completed expression goes through a few distinctive iterations. The first iteration results when seven circles complete the first beautiful form, called the Genesis Pattern. It symbolizes the beginning of life.

The second iteration integrates thirteen circles and is called the Egg of Life. In many cultures this pattern symbolizes fertility and rebirth. It is the shape that births the Flower of Life.

As a symbol, the Flower of Life represents the Universe as a whole, our understanding of our connection to it, and how all the separate yet interdependent components of the Universe work together. It is an expression of our understanding that everything is connected, that nothing is separate or coincidental. Everything is part of the whole. Including you and me. And every component of the whole is, itself, a whole, capable of creativity and development to realize its evolving potential.

## The Flower of Life grounds us and demonstrates our understanding of our connection to each other and to the whole.

I'd like to imagine that the Flower of Life actually represents how we as individuals are all connected at our centers, our hearts. We already saw how we each have an energy field around us that is made of our thoughts and our feelings. It is our personal bubble, and we can imagine it as a perfect circle in which we are whole and complete by ourselves. Our hearts are at the center of this bubble.

When we make a connection with someone else and resonate with them, we connect in our heart centers . . . right in the middle of our energy bubbles. We connect through love: the love we have for ourselves, which helps us maintain our integrity, and the love we have for one another, which helps us maintain the integrity of relationships. We can imagine that as we make multiple heart-based connections with others, we ultimately create a pattern like the Flower of Life.

If we continue to add people to our heart connections and thus add circles to the pattern, it will eventually form a Flower of Life grid that can reach all over the world! That is the magic of our magic; when we all individually spark our own magic by creating a beautiful bubble of coherence between mind and body (thoughts and feelings), we can then together create a magical world of co-creation between us and in collaboration with a higher power, both as individuals and as networks of mindful people.

## Bridge into the Subconscious

We saw that sacred geometry is the blueprint of creation and even the structuring pattern at the essence of *you*. Because it is at the very core of your being—including your DNA, your cells, and your atoms— you recognize sacred geometry as a language on a subconscious level, even if that information is not encoded in words. It can spark an instant (unconscious) feeling of harmony, belonging, and inner peace. You feel the coherence and creative orderliness that is the hallmark of sacred geometry at work.

Remember that we discovered the subconscious makes up around 90 percent of your mind? And that who you are mostly derives from the habits and beliefs buried in the depths of your subconscious?

Those habits and beliefs are at the core of your thoughts and feelings. They therefore give rise to the energy you generate and thus the signal you send out to the Universe with your "wish list." You'll recognize the habits and beliefs that limit you because they'll feel "out of tune" with sacred geometry. Developing your awareness of what's in tune and what's out of tune, something that you're doing whenever you enter Perceptual Mode, will help you align your energy so that you can express your full potential and work the magic that is your life.

# To make real changes we have to address the subconscious.

To align your thoughts and feelings—and therefore your energy—with your true vision and desires, you will have to dive into the abyss of the mysterious subconscious. You need to change the out-of-tune programs that are running your behavior and thus determining your energy and what you attract. You cannot expect changes in what you cause and create if you keep having the same thoughts and the same feelings that generate the same energy. If you want to change what and who you attract, you have to send a different signal into the Universe. You have to change your energy bubble by thinking new thoughts and generating new feelings. You have to be different to create something different. And being different involves addressing what is buried in your subconscious.

All that sounds wonderfully simple in theory, right? But how do you *get* to all the stuff that is stored outside the reach of your conscious mind? How do you get past the barrier of the analytical mind?

## Sacred Geometry Design

To get out of your 3D thinking and access your subconscious, you need to bypass your conscious mind. When we shift into Perceptual Mode through meditation, we experience this movement from the conscious to the subconscious mind. In meditation we close our eyes and draw our attention inward and away from the 3D world that is governed by our senses, so we can access the realm of the subconscious and the soul.

Plato called sacred geometry "the language of the soul."

Another way of bypassing the conscious mind is to induce a trance-like state while staying awake.

By giving our eyes something to look at that has no reference to the 3D world, we bypass our thinking minds and open a direct pathway into the subconscious. If we use sacred geometry imagery, the effects are even more powerful, as our subconscious intrinsically feels at home in the realm of divine architecture. Sacred geometry can reach between multidimensionality and the mundane 3D world, between the conscious and the subconscious minds.

For thousands of years, sacred geometry has been a part of every culture. It is the bond that connects us all to the cosmos; it is the true design of our souls. Sacred geometric principles have been used in ancient mandalas found in many cultures in both the East and the West, such as Hinduism, Buddhism, and even Christianity, where the form of the Celtic cross reflects these principles most clearly. These designs were used as tools to meditate, focus, and create sacred space. It is remarkable how people on different continents all discovered the same thing: that the power of mandalas—and sacred geometry—can support us in accessing a deeper level of consciousness. The Sri Yantra mandala is an example of this and has been used for centuries as a symbol to represent the cosmos and the union between the Divine Masculine and the Divine Feminine.

In the modern world, people use mandalas in meditation, Chinese medicine, Reiki, feng shui, and other disciplines. Jung studied mandalas and incorporated them into his work, having patients create their own mandalas so they could experience wholeness and connection to the sacred, and many therapists and healers continue to use mandalas in this way. I use sacred geometry to create "modern-day mandalas" to inspire original thought and activate thinking

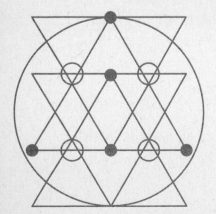

beyond the everyday so we can make real changes in our lives. You'll find more about this practice in the end of this book.

# Tune In

Before we go into Perceptual Mode, take a piece of paper and cut out six squares, six triangles, and six circles. Keep these shapes close to you.

Follow your breath into Perceptual Mode. Take the shapes you just cut out and move them around until they fall into a pattern that feels pleasing or harmonious to you. You can use all of them or only some of them.

Looking at the pattern you created, allow concepts or words to arise that describe this composition and your experience of it: peaceful, creative, chaotic, flowing, balanced, and so on.

Keep in mind your composition and its meaning to you while you contemplate the words of Galileo Galilei from the beginning of this chapter:

> [The Universe] cannot be read until we have learnt the language and become familiar with the characters in which it is written. It is written in mathematical language, and the letters are triangles, circles and other geometrical figures, without which means it is humanly impossible to comprehend a single word.

Journal about what you have discovered in your exploration of sacred geometry. You may want to photograph your mandala and keep it for further contemplation.

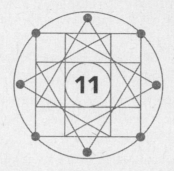

# ENERGY MANAGEMENT:
# THE POWER OF BOUNDARIES

*Step with care and great tact, and remember that*
*life's a great balancing act.*

DR. SEUSS, AUTHOR

We now know that everything is energy and that all energy organizes itself according to the same universal laws in repeating patterns and grids. We also understand that our thoughts and our feelings are energy and that they are at the core of our magical power, our ability to deliberately cause and create outcomes. We discovered that many of these thoughts and feelings are generated by beliefs buried deep inside our subconscious, where they are turned into programs that run our automatic behavior and responses. And often these beliefs are not in alignment with what we want to create for ourselves.

To break the cycles of automatic responses and repetitive behavior we need to first and foremost become *aware* of them. Unless we recognize when we are triggered into an automatic emotional response and are willing to look at it, we will continue to repeat the same behavior, leading to the same thoughts and the same feelings that then cause the same outcome, that then leads to the same behavior, and so on. However, when we are conscious of how we feel, we have the opportunity to dive into the depths of our inner world and dig for the buried treasure of unresolved experiences. I call this "treasure" because of the enormous value the discovery of unresolved issues and experiences can offer. When energy is bound up in what is unresolved, and we resolve these experiences, we free up energy for us to use deliberately and creatively. Bringing these experiences to the surface where they can be seen, understood, and let go of, we release energy and make room for new ways of thinking and feeling . . . and ultimately, new ways of being. And as we discovered earlier, it is our way of being that determines the vibration—the "wish list"—that we send out into the Universe. Our emotions are our most important guidance to show us where to start looking.

## Emotions

We are all capable of feeling a wide variety of emotions, from happiness, joy, and pleasure to sadness, anger, fear, and disgust, and anything in between. An emotion is much more than "a feeling," though, since it often includes physical reactions and behaviors as well, like how you laugh out loud when you are happily surprised, how you yell at someone when you are angry, or how your heart races when you feel fear or excitement.

So, what exactly are emotions, and why are they so important?

Let's start by looking at the word itself. The word "emotions" can be considered as e-motions, where the "e" refers to energy and "motion" to the movement of it.

# Emotions are energy in motion.

Emotions can be described as the movement of energy through the body, causing a combination of feelings, physical reactions, and behaviors. Emotions also resonate throughout our multidimensional selves, threading their way through every level of consciousness and affecting us at every level of awareness: they are patterns of energy that affect our whole selves.

We already saw that we are vibrational beings, made of energy. Our emotions are a powerful built-in navigational system that can help us become aware of where our energy flows and where it is blocked. Since e-motions are energy in motion, we can increase our awareness of energy by following our emotions, and thus learn to move energy, dissolve energetic blocks, and make new energetic connections.

Much of the input for the way we perceive the world comes from our feelings and our emotions. Our emotions help us to decide what to do, where to look, what to stay away from, what to remember, and what to do next. We often steer ourselves in the direction of the things that attract us and move away from the things that don't. What attracts us is what we feel aligned with—what makes us feel good, happy, and excited. By becoming aware of our emotions, we can adjust our course of action accordingly and appropriately.

Think about this: When you are happy—when you are in love, for instance—you feel like you're bursting with energy. The energy is flowing freely through your body, often crashing through blocks and obstacles along the way. When you are in this state of being, you feel like you can take on anything and often can barely remember why you were concerned with anything challenging. Pain can magically disappear, and the problems you thought you couldn't overcome all of a sudden appear to only be small bumps in the road. In this joyful state of being you *attract* people and circumstances that match your happy energy, and you *feel attracted* to more of what enhances or continues this joyful state of being; you might find yourself wanting to listen to upbeat happy music, watch fun and romantic movies, and share the company of people who are happy and joyful as well. As the energy is flowing freely through your body, you are literally "turned on," causing your vibration to rise and your whole being to light up.

## Turn On, Turn Off

Let's explore what being "turned on" really means from an energy point of view.

We are made of energy: we are vibrational beings, and like electrical circuit boards, we can literally light up when energy freely flows through us. Being "turned on" actually expands far beyond the narrow definition of being sexually aroused. Being "turned on" is a state of being that certainly *can* be achieved through sexual arousal, but there are other ways to achieve the same free flow of energy through the body and the attendant physical, emotional, and chemical responses. (The release of feel-good hormones, the activation of the body's self-healing ability, and the inability to think linear thoughts are some of them.) You can achieve this state through meditation, whether you use it to shift into Perceptual Mode or as a contemplative practice. You can also focus on sacred geometry and go into a wakeful trance. Accomplishing something amazing, like running a marathon or making a groundbreaking scientific discovery, can also catapult us into the higher energy vibrations of being turned on.

When we understand that we are patterns of energy, we can see that being turned on affects much more than just the physical body. Our optimal brightness derives from all parts of us being turned on, or being open to a free flow of energy, or being aligned with our purpose and soulselves. When this happens, all aspects of our beings align and harmonize: physical, emotional, spiritual, and mental. This enables us to express ourselves creatively across all domains.

The opposite happens as well; when you feel sad or angry, you often feel drained. Your energy is not free-flowing; instead, it is blocked and slow. Just think about how you breathe more shallowly and even hold your breath completely when you are sad, or how you clench your jaw or your fists when you are angry. This tension prevents energy from flowing freely through your body, and your light literally dims. Imagine yourself again as an electrical circuit board. When there are disconnects between circuits, the energy flow is disrupted, and things don't light up. This is the same with the body. When we get angry, we tense up and the energy no longer flows. This is not a problem if it is temporary, and ideally this is how it should work: the emotion arises and shows us that there

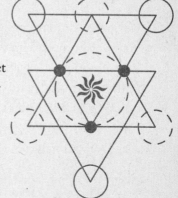

is something to look at, and we address the cause, resolve it, let it go, and allow the energy to flow freely again. Unfortunately, this is often not how it goes. Often the emotion arises and we don't know what to do with it or how to resolve it, or we might not even be consciously aware of how we feel at all. So, we don't address it. This way many of our feelings and experiences go unresolved and end up buried in our subconscious, where they become part of the programs that run our (unconscious) behavior and ways of being.

# Emotions help us become aware of how we feel, what works, and what does not work, so we can make adjustments.

There are many ways we can generate energetic blocks if we are unaware of our programming or our emotions. Even apparently positive emotions that align us more strongly with our programming (rather than with our true selves) can create blocks, but by far, the emotion that generates the majority of our blocks is fear. Fear can paralyze us, stop us from thinking clearly, and make us act in ways that are not in alignment with our well-being.

# Understanding Fear

Fear is the emotion you feel when you (think that you) are in danger of being harmed, hurt, or killed, either physically or psychologically. The threat can be real or imagined.

Fear is a primitive and natural emotion that serves a very important role in keeping you safe. When you feel you are in danger, fear causes your brain to signal your body to go into "fight or flight" mode, so you can either stay and deal with the threat or run away to safety. This is important, because when you are in danger you need your body to function optimally, even if the temporary boost comes with a cost later. Running or fighting takes energy, so the body shuts down functions that are not needed for this and instead directs all energy to dealing with or avoiding the threat. In response to acute stress, your endocrine system releases adrenaline, which triggers your heart to beat faster, which pumps more blood through your body, which gives your muscles more energy. Your pupils dilate so more light can come in and improve your vision. Your skin becomes paler as blood is redirected to your muscles. During this state of crisis, all non-essential functions are reduced or postponed. Digestion is suspended, and so is your immune system, as you are choosing to survive in the moment rather than avoid getting sick in the future. The blood flow to your brain is directed to the parts that support survival behavior instead of the part of the brain that supports the ability to think straight. That's why when we're afraid we can act without thinking; our automatic survival mechanism takes over.

Now, this whole system is designed to be a quick response to a temporary situation. When you are being chased by angry bees, being threatened at gunpoint, or hanging from a cliff over a ravine, you need your body to do whatever it takes to get you to safety. All your resources and energy have to be directed at getting you out of danger. Once you are safe you can start your recovery, meaning your body can direct energy back to the digestive system, the immune system, and restorative sleep.

Unfortunately, in today's world, many of us live in a constant state of stress, anxiety, and fear. We hardly ever return fully to a resting or unaroused state, either at a psychological level or at a hormonal level.

## Real or Not Real?

We all have things we are afraid of besides immediate threats. Some might be frightening to almost all of us, while other triggers can be very personal. Fear of death, sickness, losing someone we love, and not having enough money to survive are pretty common for many, while being alone, getting old, the dark, water, spiders, dogs, bees, or lightning can be terrifying for some of us and absolutely okay for others. Our fears are very much part of our personal realities.

Some fears find their roots in past experiences, while others are based on the stories and beliefs of others, our cultures, our religions, or other social constructs. Many fears are 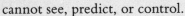 about things in the future that we cannot see, predict, or control.

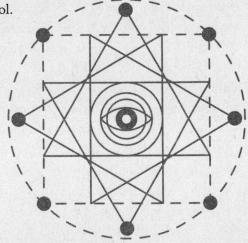

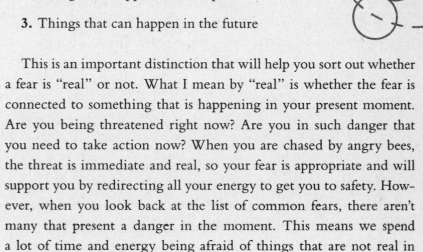

We can divide fear into three categories:

**1.** Things that are happening now

**2.** Things that happened in the past

**3.** Things that can happen in the future

This is an important distinction that will help you sort out whether a fear is "real" or not. What I mean by "real" is whether the fear is connected to something that is happening in your present moment. Are you being threatened right now? Are you in such danger that you need to take action now? When you are chased by angry bees, the threat is immediate and real, so your fear is appropriate and will support you by redirecting all your energy to get you to safety. However, when you look back at the list of common fears, there aren't many that present a danger in the moment. This means we spend a lot of time and energy being afraid of things that are not real in the moment—things that are taking away our focus and energy from our magic, our ability to create outcomes that are aligned with our visions and desires.

## The Unknown

Almost all fears that are about things in the future derive from a general unease with "the unknown." We simply don't like not being able to see where we are going or what is going to happen. We don't like unpredictability and uncertainty, and the future is full of exactly that. It's like driving through thick mist and not knowing if we are going to crash into something at any moment, or if the road is ending and we will find ourselves falling off the end of the world. For many of us this is an appropriate metaphor for how we feel while trying to navigate our lives. And all the unknowns and uncertainties cause a constant state of fear and anxiety.

A large part of what generates this fear of the unknown is the fact that we don't really understand how things work. Our current belief systems and paradigms do not cover the way the Universe works, how life creates itself, how everything is energy, how like attracts like, that change is the only certainty, and how we fit into the whole kaleidoscope of vibrational patterns and repetitions. Few of us enter into Perceptual Mode, which gives us insight into the way the Universe operates. But when we *do* enter Perceptual Mode, we experience uncertainty as inviting curiosity and openness, something that encourages us to become aware rather than vigilant. Uncertainty is a gateway to multidimensional reality. Multidimensionality is still a term that is mostly known only in esoteric, metaphysical, and scientific circles, not something that is being taught in schools to help us build a model of our world that puts us in a co-creational relationship with the quantum field. We are not taught to approach everything from an energetic and vibrational point of view to help us understand our role in what unfolds in our lives. We are not trained to build our tolerance for the openness of uncertainty, which allows us to practice magic. We compartmentalize everything instead of operating from a perspective of inclusion and interconnection between all that is. We cut ourselves off from our relationship to the essential creativity of the Divine.

This outdated model of ourselves and our connection to the whole puts us outside of the Divine and does not acknowledge our power to create with it. No wonder we feel alone and afraid. We are taught that a higher power is outside of us and we are left down here basically stumbling around in the dark, hoping to be rewarded for "good behavior." This dynamic is common to all our limiting programs and the beliefs that sustain them. We are terrified that if we do something "wrong" we will be punished. We don't realize that our way of being—and thus our energy—attracts people and circumstances into our lives.

## Ultimately all fear comes down to our fear of being alone, separated from Source.

When we recognize that we are, in fact, in co-creation with the Universe, we don't have to be afraid anymore. On the contrary, as active participants in the unfolding of what and who shows up in our lives, we realize that we are modern magicians and that the quantum field is an exciting place full of potential and magic that we cannot wait to dive into!

## Sorting Things Out

Everything is made of energy. Our ability to deliberately co-create our lives is directly related to our ability to recognize, work, direct, and manage energy, on all levels and in all domains of our lives. It all starts with becoming aware of where we direct our energy and why.

Look at it this way: we all have 100 percent of our energy to work with. Now we can make deliberate choices about how we want to use that energy and how we are going to recharge it when we run low. How you spend your energy is a very personal choice; you might choose to spend 60 percent on work, 20 percent on relationships, 10 percent on self-care, and 10 percent on everything else. Your friend, on the other hand, might choose to spend 80 percent on work, 10 percent on exercise, 5 percent on travel, and 5 percent on relationships. There is no right or wrong here; they are all personal choices about how we want to fill in the details of our lives. What is important, though, is to be aware of how we feel while we are doing things so that we can allocate our energy and attention to what enables us to express our potential.

You can basically ask these three questions with anything you do:

**1.** Is what I am doing giving me energy?

**2.** Is what I am doing taking energy away?

**3.** Is what I am doing neutral to my energy level?

When it comes to relationships with others, things can get especially blurry as far as why we seek them, maintain them, stay in them, or end them. Since we are not taught that we are part of the Divine, that we each carry a piece of divinity inside us and that we are infinite and never end, we are afraid to be alone. So, we look outside ourselves for connections with others.

Sometimes the desire to connect is motivated by curiosity or attraction that emerges when we recognize someone who can help us see ourselves more clearly or support us to grow more fully into our authentic selves. These kinds of relationships can be mutually beneficial: the giving and receiving of energy often flows both ways and, ultimately, we gain energy from them.

Sometimes we look for company to escape a feeling of scarcity; we're trying to get what we feel we lack, forgetting that we are sufficient in and of ourselves. This kind of relationship is often based in

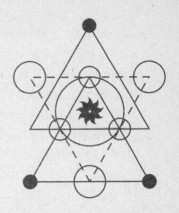

need instead of creation and in the long run will take more energy than it generates.

Sometimes we are open to connecting with others not because we are tending to our own energy but because we want to help them, we find them attractive, or we are enjoying their company. This kind of relationship is pretty neutral and often happens when we feel we have plenty of energy to give to someone else.

Sometimes we're not even aware that we've connected with someone or that their energy has an effect on ours until we consciously tune in to see what is going on with our energy levels.

Take a moment and think about a few of the most prominent relationships in your life. How would you "rate" them using the three questions about energy (is the relationship giving you energy, taking it away, or neutral)? It is important to be aware of what's happening with your energy, both when you are filled up and when you feel it draining away.

## Follow your joy.

A great way of navigating your relationships—and your life, for that matter—is to follow your joy. Joy is the emotion with the highest vibration, meaning that it can light us up as no other feeling can. As a general rule you should do more of what gives you joy and less of what doesn't. If you are in a relationship that constantly causes you stress, irritation, or discomfort, then perhaps you should ask yourself why you are staying in it. Perhaps there is still something to discover about yourself? Or perhaps you are maintaining the relationship because you are too afraid to leave?

When we recognize the patterns in our lives, we can be deliberate in how we engage with others energetically.

## Overwhelm

We have all been there: You have been running around like a superhero, tending to work, your partner, and your children; doing groceries and housework; maintaining relationships with your friends and family; keeping up with social media and the news; and squeezing in a workout or yoga session here and there. And then all of a sudden, you feel completely exhausted and drained. You simply cannot get out of bed or gather yourself to show up for that lunch that you had planned with a friend. You cannot even find the energy to check your social media anymore. Everything seems too much. You are overwhelmed.

Being overwhelmed means that you are taking in more than you can process. It also means that you are using more energy (physical or emotional) than you can generate to keep up with everything.

You are an energetic being, and 100 percent of your energy is available to use. It is imperative that you stay in tune with your energy level and are aware of when you lose energy, when you gain energy, and when you stay neutral. When you find yourself low on energy, you will have to honor that and focus on recharging yourself. You also need to learn how to set boundaries to prevent your energy level from getting so low that you reach a state of overwhelm. Even in your relationship with your higher self, the Divine, God, or the Universe, you need to be in tune with how much input you can receive and when you need to withdraw to tend to yourself. Just because you are in tune with all the whispers that come from the subtle realms doesn't mean that you have to always be listening to them. The Universe offers constant input; it does not consider the limitations that we human beings have on how much we can handle—both negative and positive. Sometimes a complete (temporary) disconnect from everything is in order, to get us back into balance.

## (Self-)Sabotage

We often sabotage our own evolution and growth. All the programs that are buried in our subconscious prompt us to create the same scenarios over and over again. If, in the past, we've allowed people with dysfunctional energies and patterns into our space, we might seek new connections and relationships that have the same dysfunctional qualities. This happens because the original experience that generated pain and distress was not resolved and is now buried deep in the subconscious, where it generates an automatic program that keeps us locked in the same pattern. Even though we *know* better, we can't help but be run by our subconscious.

Another way we self-sabotage is when we are actually doing fantastic—we are going beyond our previous states of happiness, success, or abundance—and we create something (a disaster, sickness, failure) to slow ourselves down. We are so used to the lower energies of our "old" state of being that we become paralyzed by the potential of success. It's so much easier to stay small and dream of what we want than to risk failure by pursuing it—or to achieve our dreams and face the uncertainty that follows.

## Empathy

We discovered in chapter 5 that as vibrational beings who are in tune with all that is, we can easily tune in to other people's energy. While this kind of tuning in is incredibly valuable to help us get a complete picture of our reality (remember that reality is our perception of our inner and our outer worlds), it can also "backfire" a bit on us when we don't only *tune in* to other people but *take on* their energy and thus their emotions as well.

When we are being deliberate, we shift into Perceptual Mode and allow our inner guidance to give us feedback and insights about the other person without crossing over boundaries to enter into their experience. This is healthy and creates a strong foundation for relationships.

However, when we're not deliberate, we can unintentionally absorb others' fears and blocks just by being near them. Like we saw in chapter 5, when we are close to another person, our energy bubbles overlap, and we can (unconsciously) pick up on each other's thoughts and feelings. We can leave our own experience and enter theirs, absorbing the energies, blocks, and turbulence of their programming, fears, and beliefs. When you take on other people's energy in addition to your own, you can block the flow of your energy. For example, when you have unresolved fears and limiting beliefs buried in your subconscious, interacting with someone who is fearful or in pain will trigger your programming to generate feelings of fear and limitation in you. If the person you're with is arguing for the 3D paradigm, which is defined by limitations, you can also block the flow of your own energy by forgetting your origin, your soulself. When you are out of alignment with your own energy and your connection to Source is weakened by your fears, by your limiting beliefs, or by empathetic acceptance of someone else's fears or beliefs, you may feel overwhelmed, sabotage yourself, or generate limitations that will keep you "comfortable" by keeping you on familiar ground.

When we're deliberate, we perceive others more accurately, and we don't simply absorb their energy. With practice, we can sort out our distortions from theirs and merely *perceive* how they are feeling, what is going on with them, if they are authentic and honest (with us), or even if they are hiding something. This is true even if they are unaware of their own stories and distortions.

## Tune In

Read through what follows once so you get the gist of what we are trying to do. It doesn't matter whether you are doing it exactly as described here. The most important thing to get from this is that your intention is to pull your awareness away from the outside world for a few minutes and allow that which doesn't serve you anymore to leave you, while you fill yourself up with light.

Follow your breath into Perceptual Mode and move your awareness inward, tuning in to your energy and allowing it to flow.

▲ Close your eyes if that feels comfortable for you. Take a deep breath. In through the nose, hold it for a second, and then out through the mouth. Let's do it again: in through the nose, hold it, and out through the mouth. Ahhhhhh.

▲ Come on into that beautiful, coherent place, your heart center, breathing softly yet deeply.

▲ Allow the outside world to just fade away for a moment.

▲ Tune in to your heart space and feel it. How does it feel? Does it feel open? Closed? Contracted? Peaceful? Restless?

▲ Tune further inward and observe your emotions for a moment. How do you feel? What word comes to mind? Don't overthink it; just go with the first impression that comes up.

▲ Scan your body or your inner being—is there any part that draws your attention? Any pains? Discomfort? Tension? Stress? Where do you feel it?

▲ Now imagine that you are standing somewhere you feel really connected to the Universe. This could be on top of a mountain, by the ocean, or in the forest.

▲ Imagine yourself standing there with your arms wide open, your eyes closed.

▲ Now imagine a bright beam of light coming down, pouring over you and filling you up. All you need to do is just stand there and take it in. The light washes over you like a shower.

▲ Imagine it filling you up, starting to flow from your head down into your whole body. When you get to the places that feel tense or painful, pause for a moment and imagine those spots filling up with light, washing out anything that doesn't serve you anymore. Just let it flow away, out of your body, out of your being, into the earth where it will be transmuted into light. Notice what is being carried away in this flow of light. Do you see your own fears and beliefs in limitations or scarcity? Do you see energy you've absorbed from other people?

▲ Slowly come back to the physical world. Notice your heart beating or your breath going in and out to guide you back.

In your journal, you might record what you came to understand about your own limiting fears and beliefs and how the energy from other people creates obstacles in your flow. How might you use Perceptual Mode to transform these limiting beliefs and release blockages created by other people's energy?

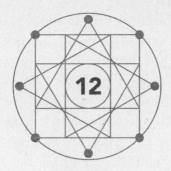

# TOOLS:
# THE POWER OF DOING

*Life is like riding a bicycle. To keep your balance you must keep moving.*

**ALBERT EINSTEIN, THEORETICAL PHYSICIST**

The quote by Albert Einstein holds so much truth. Not only is it a reflection of the essence of the Universe (forever moving, changing, and morphing), but it is also a reminder that we are never really stuck, and that as long as we understand that energy wants to move, we can make different decisions and take new actions in each moment. Even when we don't see how or when things will change, what is unarguably true is that if we keep repeating the same behavior and thinking the same thoughts, we will continue to have the same feelings, which then keep us in the same patterns. The saying "the definition of insanity is doing the same thing over and over again and expecting a different result" is a great illustration of this. Making a move, changing something—anything—to break a pattern is a worthy step toward your co-creational power. Even simply reminding yourself that all things are always changing can help you avoid repeating the same patterns; instead, you will perceive the possibilities of different patterns emerging.

Now, let's get practical and explore tools. Some can help you keep your awareness of multidimensionality and work within that framework to shift, clear, maintain, and generate energy so you can live in a balanced state of being and stay in touch with the deep complementarity that organizes reality and supports creativity. Some will help you return to Perceptual Mode when you have fallen back into 3D thinking, which everyone does from time to time since the dominant culture still operates from that perspective. The more time you spend in Perceptual Mode, and the more environments and interactions you sustain it in, the more your vibration is amplified in everyday 3D reality; that's how systemic change happens organically and creatively.

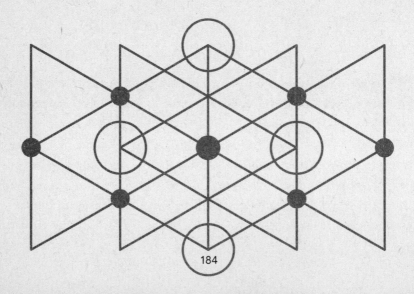

## Ceremony and Ritual

Ceremony and ritual can be of great support in creating an energetic container in which we deliberately co-create with the Universe and perform our magic. The purpose of ceremony and ritual is to awaken our awareness of the subtle realms of multidimensionality and enable us to have a common experience of those realms. In many cultures, one of the explicit goals of ceremony and ritual is to restore harmony within the individual and the community. In other words, ceremony and ritual could be seen as activities that align us with the sacred geometry, creativity, and wholeness of Source. Ceremony can be as simple as burning a candle, putting on a specific outfit, or setting up your environment or space in preparation for performing your magic.

# Clearing Your Space and Your Energy

There are some great tools that can help you *clean up* energy, clarifying the field you're centered in. Just like you use solvents and disinfectants to clean your space physically, there are powerful tools to clean your space energetically. Because just like your space (and you) can attract physical things like dust and dirt and things you don't want, you can attract energetic things that you don't want either.

For example, you may have picked up elements of your friend's bad mood by wanting to comfort them, and their sadness or disappointment came home with you unnoticed. You've caught a kind of energetic flu. Because your energy field and their energy field overlapped while in each other's presence, your energies mixed and now you are feeling (some of) what they were feeling. Or perhaps your friend came to visit you and left some of their bad mood behind in your space (your home or office).

## Just as physical disease is contagious, so is energetic dis-ease.

How can you clear the energy, either in your space or in yourself?

While you can, of course, randomly clear energy whether you are aware of something being off or not, it will serve you in the long run to learn to tune in and assess whether there is a need to cleanse and clear the energy. The first and foremost thing is that you become aware of your energy and the energy around you so you can recognize when something is not in alignment with you.

Switching to Perceptual Mode to assess your energy, your emotions, and anything else that comes up can become just as much part of your routine as assessing your physical body to see what needs attending to there. When you feel something is off, you can tune in to the subtle and energetic aspects of yourself to see what you need to get back to a balanced state, just like you consider what to do when you feel a cold coming on.

There are many different methods and tools you can use to clear energy. Which one to use is a personal choice; one is not better than any other. There are some that have been traditionally used throughout history in many different cultures, though, which could be considered an indication of their power and effectiveness.

Let's take a look at some of them.

## Smudging

Burning dried sage or any other herb or resin, also known as *smudging*, is one of the most commonly known ways to clear spaces and ourselves of negative energy. In this method we use the smoke to "cleanse" the energy. I am sure you have actually witnessed this before in churches, where incense is burned for this exact reason.

The most well-known method is to burn dried white sage. Sage is part of the salvia plant family. The name is derived from the Latin *salvere*, which means "to heal." Besides clearing negative energy, smudging has traditionally been used to promote healing and wisdom.

In the case of sage, the dried leaves are tied together in a bundle that is called a smudge stick. The stick is lit at the end and the flame quickly blown out, so that the smudge stick only smokes. The smoke is then used to cleanse the energy by walking around the space or person and wafting it everywhere.

Because smells are so strong, enabling us to retrieve apparently forgotten memories in great detail, a smell can be a very efficient tool for entering into and sustaining Perceptual Mode. You might associate a particular smudge with the practice you use to strengthen your awareness. Simply lighting a smudge stick or incense when you return to your home or before you go to bed can set up a cleansing routine that has the added bonus of adding something beautiful to your daily experience.

## Sound

Since everything is energy and all energy exists as a vibration, we can use sound to clear our spaces and ourselves of negative energy as well. Just like smudging, the use of sound vibration for cleansing dates back thousands of years, across cultures. Some of the most

well-known methods include Tibetan bells and singing bowls, ton-
ing, singing, chanting, and other forms of music.

While singing bowls and bells are beautiful, you can use anything
that makes a noise that feels beautiful, harmonious, or resonant to
you. Try flicking an empty wine glass, beating a drum, banging on a
table, clapping your hands, ringing a bell, or using your voice. Basically, you want to break up the existing energy in a space (or around
you or within you) and make it move so it can find a new, more harmonious pattern that is aligned with your well-being.

There are many powerful tuning instruments that vibrate on a specific frequency to stimulate harmony and healing. For instance, you
can get a tuning fork that resonates at 528 Hz, which is believed to
help with DNA repair. And, as with smells, you can associate sounds
with your Perceptual Mode practice both to amplify that practice and
to enhance the work of the sound.

## Crystals

Crystals have been used throughout history as powerful cleansers
and supporters of energy, both for physical spaces and for personal
energy. Crystals are solid formations of molecules that have arranged
themselves in certain repeating grid patterns. They are wonderful
examples of the many beautiful forms that sacred geometry can generate. Table salt is an example that we all know; so are snow crystals.
Each crystal has a specific formation and therefore a unique vibration.
Interestingly, crystals form out of chaotic states (sound familiar?)—
sometimes out of the apparently still chaos of a liquid, and sometimes
out of the more dynamic chaos of heat and pressure.

Many people assign great healing and other powers to crystals.
While there are certain attributes and qualities assigned to specific
crystals, the use of crystals is very personal. Remember that energies
create qualities or properties as they interact interdependently: each

person's vibration may amplify different qualities in the energy of a crystal. You can choose a crystal on the basis of research or you can allow yourself to be guided by intuition. Picking one that speaks to you, attracts you, or simply is the most beautiful to you is a great way of choosing. If you access Perceptual Mode, you will have a greater awareness of the crystal's potential to support you in healing or using your magic.

Crystals can be worn on the body as jewelry or placed in our homes and spaces to support the energy there.

## Intention

While all the above methods can be powerful tools to help you clear the energy in yourself and your space, you can do it without any of them. Just as magicians and sorcerers use the power of their intention in combination with words to alter the nature of their reality, you can do the same. You can use your focused intention and your words to direct the energy inside and around you. You can clear your own energy field or the space around you by directing energy with visualization and imagination. And to bring even more power to bear, you can use your words. All you need to do is be deliberate, unwavering, and clear. Remember that the more focused your attention is the more powerful your magical abilities are. In fact, using intention in tandem with any other tool will amplify its healing, clarifying, or cleansing effect. And operating from Perceptual Mode will clarify and strengthen your intention.

For instance, you can imagine that you have a gigantic energetic vacuum cleaner that you are going to use to suck up anything in your field or space that doesn't serve you. To make your intention really clear, state what you are doing out loud as well. Words are containers for energy, and by saying out loud what you are doing you give even more power to your intention.

For instance, you could say out loud: "I *demand* [remember, you are a powerful magician, unwavering in your conviction] that anything that doesn't serve me and my highest good leave me or my space *now*!"

To make it really clear that you mean business, you could add: "I *demand* that anything—in any of my bodies, my space, or my cells, in any dimension, in any time, in any place or space or anywhere—that has any kind of effect on me and does not serve my highest good or contribute to my optimal well-being . . . leave me *now*!"

As a multidimensional being who understands that your magic comes from your relationship with the multidimensional reality of the Universe, you want to be as inclusive as possible of anything you can think of that can have an influence on you. Not just here in your physical body, but also in your mental, emotional, or spiritual bodies; not just here on earth but everywhere else; and not just now, but through all timelines, past, present, and future.

Sometimes I use my hands and arms to wave around me, pull energy out of me, and throw it away from me; I imagine that I am sweeping, wiping, vacuuming, or combing energy out of my space; sometimes I jump, dance, or shake my body to allow energy to leave me; sometimes I spin in circles to eject energy away from me; sometimes I use imaginary scissors to cut energetic cords between me and others; and sometimes I sit still and just do it all in silence.

You can do it any way you feel like; the most important part is that your intention is strong, clear, and directed. The great thing about working with energy like this is that you can do this anywhere and anytime. You don't have to wait until you have access to tools like sage, singing bowls or bells, crystals, or anything else. You are a powerful magician in control of your own energy. And remember that joy is an indicator of being in alignment with your creative powers and those of the Universe. If dancing like a wild thing and howling while you do it gives you a feeling of joy, you've found a great way to express and amplify your intention to show up as fully and powerfully and creatively as you can.

## Protecting Yourself and Your Space

We looked at why and how to clear yourself and your space from negative energy when needed. Now we'll look at setting up protection so that you don't have to do this nearly as often, or at all.

Just as you protect your physical body from germs, viruses, extreme temperatures, and things that could otherwise hurt you, you can protect your energetic part from being affected by others or your surroundings. You can wear crystals or anything else that is made for that purpose.

You can also use the power of your imagination and visualize setting up a barrier between your field and anything outside of it. This barrier can be a bubble of beautiful light—white, silver, gold, or any color that you intuit—or it can be completely made of mirrors so that you can imagine that anything that approaches and does not serve your highest good will be instantly reflected back. This is an excellent thing to do while you're in Perceptual Mode; you can even make "bubbling up" part of your regular practice routine, initiating your return to the 3D realm.

Personally, when I go into a space that has a lot of people, I often remind myself to "put my shield up." As a highly sensitive and intuitive being, I know that I easily pick up energy from others, so I consciously put up some protection. I visualize mirrors around me, or I imagine that I put myself in a giant bubble that I can see through and move in but that is impenetrable for anything that is not in alignment with my vibration.

# Meditation

Throughout this book I have referenced meditation numerous times as a powerful tool to use when we want to go beyond our linear, thinking minds. Besides the kind of Perceptual Mode and tune-in exercises you've learned in this book, other meditation practices could include prayer and visualization. All these methods can help guide your awareness from the outer world to the inner world and slow down your brain activity, resulting in a powerful shift in your energy. You can even use Perceptual Mode as a path into the space where you pray, visualize, or work with colors or mantras.

When you are in the midst of a "bad mood," simply slowing down, or stopping what you are doing altogether, can be very effective: you might find it is one of the fastest ways to shift your energy (and, with that, your focus, the way you feel, and the thoughts you have). Even taking a few deep breaths can do wonders when you feel stressed, anxious, or angry. If you dip into Perceptual Mode as part of this process, you might even recognize what in the present triggered something from the past in your subconscious. Then you reap a double benefit: a downshift out of chaos and awareness that enables healing in the moment.

## Guided Meditation

Many tools and methods are available to help you to fine-tune your meditation. Some people prefer to meditate in absolute stillness, while others like to listen to calming sounds or music or use guided meditations. Personally, I like to use guided meditations that combine music and spoken words and that gently guide my focus and awareness away from the outside world and deeper into the realms of the subconscious and the soul. Your experience of Perceptual Mode has already given you some sense of the value of meditation, and you may find that settling into Perceptual Mode as a preliminary to more structured meditations will amplify your experience.

I start every morning with a (short) guided meditation of around twenty minutes. I do this right when I wake up; I basically roll out of bed, wrap myself in a blanket or something to keep me warm, sit down on the couch, put my AirPods in my ears, and turn on the meditation. I choose not to meditate in my bed, because it would be too easy for me to just fall back asleep. Getting myself to the couch and sitting there is a clear signal for both my body and my mind that we are starting the day and that we are doing it with a mindfulness practice. I use a soft blindfold to block all light, which makes it easier for me to drop into my inner world. Because I use a blindfold and a headset, I can easily do this meditation anywhere, even when I am traveling. My son is used to seeing me like this, and even my cats have gotten used to me not being available for them the first half hour after I wake up. Often one of them will crawl in my lap and lie there throughout my meditation.

I use a variety of guided meditations, some short, many longer (sixty to ninety minutes). Since I don't always want to dedicate time to the longer ones, I made it a part of my daily routine to at least start with the twenty-minute one right after waking up. I have found that spending a consistent twenty minutes at the beginning of my day keeps me balanced, happier, and healthier; I sleep better at night, and I feel I can cope with whatever comes my way with greater ease, grace, and humor.

I often do a longer one either in the evening or during the weekend, when my focus is less on my work.

## Moving Meditation

You don't have to sit still to go into a meditative state. Remember that the goal of meditation is to go beyond your thinking and linear mind so your brain can slow down. While sitting down and closing your eyes certainly can help you direct your focus away from the outside world and into the inner realms, it is not necessary. You can reach this state of mindfulness while doing something other than sitting as well: walking, dancing, painting, writing, drawing, doing dishes, brushing the cat, or planting flowers, for instance. Anything that has rhythm and repetition can work well for moving meditation; you might think of these actions as sacred geometry in motion. Find the proportions of movement to silence that work for you, or feel the rhythms and patterns that emerge when you do something mindfully.

I love walking meditations. I find that when my body is moving in a constant rhythm that I don't need to consciously think about, it is easy to allow my mind to relax and so enable free-flowing intuitive

thought. I often go on early evening walks like this, roaming around the neighborhood, headphones in with flowing music, having intimate time with Spirit. Of course, the exercise my body is getting this way is an extra bonus!

Some forms of yoga can be considered "moving meditation" as well. The word "yoga" is derived from Sanskrit and means union or balance. In yoga we aim to create union between the body, mind, and spirit through breath control, a set of postures, and a meditative state of mind. The often smooth flow and transitions between different postures invite the conscious mind to take a backseat for a little bit, while the breath guides the focus inward and in a mindful state.

## Meditating with Your Eyes Open

As we saw earlier, mandalas have been used for centuries as a tool for meditation. The nonconceptual nature of the designs makes them a powerful tool to go beyond the conscious mind. It's important to use nonconceptual images or visual prompts, meaning there is nothing "relatable" that the word–dependent, linear mind can latch onto and no imagery that might evoke emotional responses that derive from experiences we have gone through. There are no fluffy puppies to remind us of our childhood pets, no beautiful people who bring us back to our romantic involvements, and no sunsets or flowers that might trigger conventional 3D associations of mortality or the kind of dualistic thinking that can see a beautifully flowering plant as a weed and reject its beauty because it's judged as "bad." When we look at something that has no direct relation to any experience or habit of dualistic judgment in our lives, our minds can relax and make way for our consciousness to expand into the vast and infinite space of Spirit, nothingness, or the quantum field.

Sacred geometry can do that. Mandalas, for instance, are a way to meditate with your eyes open because they are nonconceptual images that invite your thinking mind to step aside. The sacred geometry speaks directly to your subconscious as you innately recognize the elements of the image as reflections of the divine architecture that is underneath everything. All you have to do is softly gaze at the images and allow the flow of intuitive thought. You can find more about sacred geometry and my relationship to it in the Resources section in the back of the book.

# Creativity

Creativity is the ability to create. As an inward process, it refers to the ability to make new connections between often unrelated or hidden aspects and to generate original solutions, concepts, and expressions of meaning and experience. Outwardly, it is the capacity to transform thoughts, ideas, and dreams into something tangible and real. Both processes are about the dynamics of energy—how it flows, transforms, and changes. Remembering that we are better able to perceive these dynamics with the intuitive awareness that arises in Perceptual Mode, you might choose to make Perceptual Mode part of your creative process.

When we tap into our creativity, we tap into the flow of energy within ourselves, as well as the connection between us and something larger, the Divine or Spirit. Many artists and writers affirm that their creations often seem to emerge from somewhere outside themselves and that they are merely the channel through which creative energy flows. Creativity can therefore be used to change the way we feel and think, to shift our moods. When we allow ourselves to just flow in writing, journaling, drawing, painting, or any form of creative expression, we can get beyond our thinking minds, just like in meditation.

A powerful form of creative practice is to engage in free or unstructured creativity in which the intention is to capture a *feeling* more than a *thing*. You do this by just keeping your hand moving without worrying what you are writing or drawing. You might even incorporate this sort of movement into your Perceptual Mode practice to see what emerges on paper as you observe what arises in Perceptual Mode. This way energy is flowing through you, unrestricted and undirected.

## Moving Energy inside Your Body

Sometimes we are stuck in an emotion or mood. Since emotions are energy in motion, we can shift things by literally making the energy move. Even when you feel completely paralyzed by fear, held down by depression, or stuck in sadness, you can remind yourself that moving your body will always move your *energy*, always. And moving something—anything—is better than being stuck in a feeling that you don't like.

To move our energy, we can go for a run, walk, or bike ride; we can go to the gym or take a yoga or dance class. But the fastest way to get things moving is getting up and just starting to move your body. You can jump, shake, dance, twirl, bounce, or do anything that feels good. Don't think about it; just move. You can do this anywhere at any time. Even when you find yourself at an official obligation, a presentation, a workshop, a meeting, a mall, or a party. Just find a bathroom, close the door, and do your thing to get your energy moving.

### Getting out of a Panic Attack

There are things we all can do when the fear hits us hard in a moment, like a panic attack. The first thing to do is to take a deep breath. Focusing on breathing brings you into the now moment and opens the pathway back into Perceptual Mode, where you can recognize your soulself.

Secondly, to bring you firmly into the now moment, find the following things in your environment:

▲ five things you can touch

▲ four things you can see

▲ three things you can hear

▲ two things you can taste

▲ one thing you can smell

This will engage your five senses and anchor you back into the physical realm and your body. It will help you align your 3D experience with your Perceptual Mode awareness. Your intention should be simply to focus your attention on yourself in the now, and the orderly process of locating these things will help your mind concentrate on something other than the fear.

## Gratitude

Probably one of the most powerful tools to shift our energy—and with that our moods, behaviors, and what we attract as a result—is to bring ourselves into a state of gratitude. This is powerful because true gratitude is the feeling of already having received something that you are very grateful for. It is impossible to feel gratitude without feeling that you actually received whatever you are grateful for.

# Gratitude is the ultimate state of receivership.

Our thoughts and feelings are the wish list we send into the quantum field, so being grateful for what we have is a signal to the Universe to bring us more of the same. And we can even take it a step further by being grateful for what we might not have yet, because if we can hold the vibration of feeling grateful, the signal is actually the same. The Law of Attraction, which states that like attracts like, does not differentiate between what has already happened and what we are envisioning will happen. When you feel happy and fulfilled with your vision, the energy that you are generating is the same as when you feel happy and fulfilled with the actual realization of that vision. The quantum field responds to your thoughts and feelings—the energy you send out—not to the actual manifestation.

Because we move beyond dualistic judgment and linear organizations of time in Perceptual Mode, we might find it both easier and more effective to practice gratitude if we align ourselves with the subtle energies of multidimensionality.

## Affirmations

Affirmations are positive statements (read, said, or internalized) that build up our belief in ourselves by addressing the limiting thoughts that are stored and buried in our subconscious minds. Just like we can train our physical muscles to become stronger and take on a healthier form, we can train and reshape the things we believe about ourselves, enhancing self-confidence, creativity, and productivity. Remember that it is easier for us to see what limiting thoughts or beliefs reside in our subconscious when we are in Perceptual Mode, so you might find it more effective to choose or compose affirmations from that perspective.

"I am" statements can be deeply transformative, as they can melt away the mental and emotional blocks that impede our ability to generate deep fulfillment and success in life areas like relationships, health, finance, and career. However, it is not enough to just say these statements out loud. Remember that the energy signature you send into the quantum field is a combination of both your thoughts and your feelings. For your affirmation to be most powerful, not only do you have to say the words out loud—so your mind is engaged—but you also need to *feel* that what you are saying is true and therefore real. "I am loved" does not work if you don't *feel* loved. "I am healthy" is not effective if you don't *feel* healthy. To align your feelings with these statements, imagine yourself to be what you are stating. Just like you draw people and circumstances to you that are aligned with your integrated vision, your "I am" statements need to be integrated in all that you are and feel. You may find that affirmations spoken, read, or internalized while you are in Perceptual Mode will have greater resonance and greater power.

Sacred geometry is a visual affirmation tool that supports the deep integration of fundamental human qualities with our way of being. Even better, a sacred geometry image combined with an "I am" statement activates the conscious and the subconscious at the same time: the statement addresses the conscious and subconscious minds in the linear way of words, while the image addresses the subconscious mind in a multidimensional way.

## Mind Movies

To expand on the power of affirmations, and in particular, visual affirmations, I would like to introduce you to an online tool that can support you daily in creating and manifesting your desires. Mind Movies is a platform that offers the tools to create short videos that are designed to get your mind in peak "manifesting" mode—in just a few fun minutes a day. Think of it as a digital video *vision board*, filled with positive affirmations, inspiring images, and motivating music.

The way Mind Movies works is easy and fun:

1. You *create* your own personalized Mind Movie, using easy creation software (anyone can do it, and it only takes a few minutes).

2. You *watch* your Mind Movie, and the visualization and affirmation technology naturally reprograms your subconscious mind to be in unison with your dreams and desires.

3. Your subconscious mind then works on autopilot to *manifest* your desired outcomes into reality so you can live them.

## Create it. Watch it. Live It.

If you want to experience how all this works yourself, visit https://www.mindmovies.com/.

## Forgiveness

Forgiveness is another very powerful tool to shift our energy and to make room for new thoughts and beliefs that can lead to new habits and ways of being.

## Forgiveness is the process of intentionally letting go of emotions about others or ourselves that are limiting and uncomfortable.

E-motions are energy in motion, and as part of the process of forgiveness, we move and release the energy that our feelings are holding in our bodies. Any emotion that is not properly processed has not been allowed to move through the body and out. Instead, it will be held somewhere inside the body, causing blockage in the energy flow. This can eventually lead to great discomfort and dis-ease. We solidify emotions (so they can't flow) when we label them or judge them, and we relinquish our ability to keep them moving and let them go when we assign the cause of them to something or someone outside ourselves. When we forgive others, we are also recognizing our roles as creators of our experience, which empowers us to release blocks and restore the flow of energy in the present.

By allowing this "stuck" energy to flow and leave us, we make room for something new: new thoughts, new insights, new feelings, and ultimately new ways of being.

Forgiving is a deeply personal and individual process—no one can do it for us. No one but us earns the reward of true forgiveness, either. But forgiveness from the heart can spark a profound sense of freedom and liberation, which can be deeply transformative, giving rise to new growth. One of the difficulties of forgiving is letting go of the dualistic habit of judgment. Since we move beyond dualism when we enter Perceptual Mode, we may find it much easier and more natural to forgive from that space.

## Ho'oponopono

Ho'oponopono is an ancient Hawaiian practice of forgiveness. The word Ho'oponopono means "to cause things to move back in balance" or "to make things right." Originally this could mean with our ancestors or the land, or with the people we have relationships with, including ourselves. It consists of saying four simple yet powerful lines that you direct to your focus of forgiveness. These lines represent the energies of repentance, forgiveness, gratitude, and love.

The process acknowledges that we, ourselves, are always at the center of everything that unfolds in and around us in our lives. *We* are the point of attraction and are therefore responsible for, accountable for, and in control of how we deal with, process, and resolve anything that happens in our lives. What happens to us matters not nearly as much as

203

what we do with it. Even the things that seemingly happen "outside" of ourselves can so be resolved "inside" of us.

Ho'oponopono is a powerful process that can bring balance between our inner and outer experience, and the beautiful part of it is that you don't need anybody else to be there—you can do it all by yourself. You don't need anybody to hear you. You can "say" the words in your head or out loud, visualizing the person or situation and yourself in relationship to them.

The words are simple:

1. I'm sorry . . . (fill in whatever you want to forgive for)

2. Please, forgive me

3. Thank you

4. I love you (or, you are loved, you are safe)

Carrying around resentment, anger, or pain takes a toll on our well-being, whether those feelings are about someone else or the guilt and shame we feel about something we have done ourselves. Sometimes we ourselves are the most important ones we need to forgive. This could be for not eating as healthfully as we could, drinking too much, not exercising enough, not getting enough sleep, or being unkind to our dogs, our kids, our friends, or the world—anything you would like to focus on.

## Oracle Decks

Oracle decks express humans' desire to be in touch with the Divine and with their own intuition, which is the bridge into the Divine. Humans have long sought oracles for guidance, whether those oracles be objects (*I Ching*, augury, reading tea leaves, casting runes) or people. In ancient Greece, priestesses were believed to give prophecies that were messages from the gods. These priestesses were known as oracles, wise women inspired by the gods who could give counsel or predict the future. Often this advice was mysterious, as divine guidance does not follow rules of common language and communication in linear or logical terms. After all, divine guidance emerges from multidimensional reality, so the Divine speaks in that domain's subtle language through images, metaphors, riddles, and intuition. Needless to say, we are more likely to understand what an oracle means if we are in the same domain, so entering Perceptual Mode better prepares you to read an oracle.

On our journey through this book, we have found that the Universe (or God, Spirit, the Divine, Source) communicates to us through our intuitions and it is up to us to translate and give meaning to the signals that come to us from the realms of Spirit. We connect with Source through Perceptual Mode, not by reasoning our way to it. Oracle cards can catalyze that shift and help us sustain that experience.

Oracle decks are designed to be used intuitively, so going into Perceptual Mode before you work with them will give you better insights into the possibilities they offer. Whether you draw one card or a multitude, whether you just ask a question or follow a specific drawing, the cards are meant to gently offer you an insight, a suggestion, or some food for thought: a little insight nugget to contemplate while you go through your day. Oracle decks can help you perceive how a challenge creates an opportunity. So, a specific card might help you see that what you perceive as a limitation or obstacle can actually awaken a solution or transformative response. Always. That's the complementary dynamic that magic operates through, the dynamic that is at the core of the Universe and that arises out of co-creation.

Oracle decks can make potential and possibility perceptible.

The oracle decks I have created are based on sacred geometry so that they resonate with your soul and your subconscious. And I use symbology, colors, numbers, and shapes—all "systems" that are multi-dimensional maps to help us navigate life in the physical world. And all these systems operate from the principle of complementarity, the fundamental dynamic of magic.

You can find more information about my decks in the back of the book (or on my website: https://lon-art.com).

# Transformation Tool

As a last tool and resource to support you on your journey of becoming a Modern Merlin that is in full co-creation with the Universe, I offer you the Modern Merlin Transformation Tool—a set of templates that will integrate everything that you and I discovered together into a model that will help you make sense of what is going on in your life, understand who and what is showing up and why, and learn how to align everything toward the vision that you have for yourself. I invite you to use this tool often and whenever you feel you find a limiting belief that is not aligned with your vision. The Transformation Tool will help you transform your limiting belief and strengthen and deepen your supportive beliefs.

You can find the Transformation Tool on page 225.

# Tune In

Choose any of the tools or practices described in this chapter and try it out while you are in Perceptual Mode. Consider using a journal as a kind of logbook for your exploration of the tools. You might think of it as a journal of exploration!

A basic template for a log entry might include answers to these questions:

▲ Which practice or tool did you choose?

▲ What event or experience was the catalyst for you to try the tool or practice?

▲ What did you learn in your practice session?

▲ How might you apply this to your life, in both big and small ways? (Be sure to include specifics!)

You might find it particularly useful to note the ways this tool or practice is most useful to you in a reflection on your experience:

▲ Does it feel like a good fit?

▲ Did it give you any insight into habitual reactions or ways of seeing your experience?

▲ Did it help you shift from habitual reactions to responses that show greater awareness of the situation and your true self's capacity to engage with your experience?

▲ What kinds of issues would you use this tool or practice to explore and address?

You might find that the more detail you add as you describe the experience that prompted you to use this practice or tool, the more insight you will gain into the experience and into the value of the practice. And you might be able to strengthen your skill in using the tool if you write about the process of this experimental session—how insight led to insight or how shifts in your body led to deeper shifts in your physical sense of well-being. Reviewing the process as you record it might also amplify the transformations you experienced.

## A Possible Template:

Tool or practice:

Event or experience:

Takeaways or what I learned:

How I can apply it:

Reflection:

Details about the session:

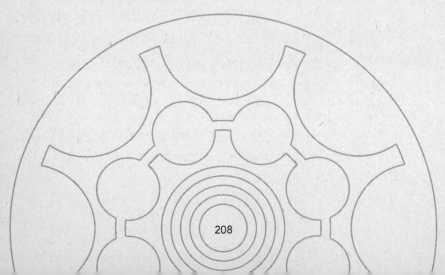

# AFTERWORD

Here you are. You have traveled all the way through this book and now you find yourself here, at a point that can be defined as an end, yet, in a multidimensional reality, everything co-exists in complementary relationship with its opposite. So, this milestone in the journey signifies as much an end as it does a new beginning—the beginning of your continuing journey into your mastery of your magic. This journey will be ever evolving and unfolding.

I wrote this book not only for you, but for myself as well. Expanding beyond what we know, integrating new perspectives, and changing habits and behaviors is a lifelong journey that never ends—for anyone, including me. We all have days in which we are more gracious than others in implementing new information into our ways of being and doing. Sometimes we are in effortless flow, while other times we feel like we are slogging through the mud and "doing the right thing" just does not feel possible. A great example of this is how we all know we should eat in a healthy way, yet—as we are human—sometimes we forget, or we just can't seem to get there, and we indulge ourselves.

The human journey is one of perfect imperfection. It is all part of being an energetic being in a physical body on earth. We are all here to learn and to become more expanded versions of ourselves, infinitely unfolding, continuously exploring, endlessly discovering and expanding, until we transition out of our physical bodies and return to Source. If we knew how to do everything, we would not need to be here (on earth) in the first place, and we surely wouldn't need a book like this.

Human nature gives us a hunger for growing, for learning, for becoming more, and especially for discovering tools to help us create lives that are fulfilling and that we are excited about while searching for depth, reason, and purpose.

I hope that I have been able to provide you with some new insights and perspectives on life and how to live it in flow. We all have magical powers; all we need to do is open ourselves to the awareness that we are on a journey of infinite discovery and growth toward full co-creational relationship with the Universe.

With Love, Light, and Magic,

# A FINAL WORD FROM THE WORLD OF ACADEMIA

In the winter of 2019, Lon asked me to coach her in developing an online course to present the *Modern Merlin* material, and I immediately recognized the transformative potential of the work, not just for me but ultimately for anyone who would engage in the process it facilitates. When Lon realized that the central themes and concepts of the course needed to be developed if they were to catalyze the kind of transformation she's committed to facilitating, she contacted her publisher. The editorial staff accepted her book proposal and validated our sense that the richness and resonance of these ideas and practices merited the kind of in-depth treatment that a book would allow. The intervening year, with its chaos and complexity, has shown how timely the release of *Modern Merlin* is. In effect, what you have in your hand is an integrative textbook for the course that emerged from Lon's experience of creating her oracle decks and Soul Portraits as well as her work in facilitating people's use of these tools to transform their understanding of themselves and their role in creating their experience of an interdependent, dynamic, and rapidly evolving world.

Writing the book gave us the opportunity to explore more fully the modalities of perceiving, thinking, and creating that Lon had begun to articulate in developing her course. As we wrote about them and the multidimensional reality that such ways of seeing reveal, we knew that we needed to do more than talk about that experience: we needed to catalyze that experience for the reader. Our first exercises were meditations that would bring the reader into what we came to call Perceptual Mode, a way of engaging intuition and insight as primary modes of knowing. As we continued writing our way into chapters on Magic, Time, Reality, Energy, Soul, and Vision and Purpose, we found that returning to Perceptual Mode at the end of every chapter was necessary if people were to make these insights their own. So, each chapter presents concepts (like magic or energy) as they have evolved to become paths to explore multidimensionality and closes with an activity specifically designed to catalyze an experience that invites readers to take their own journey into this newly emergent reality.

To support Lon in the exposition of ideas and concepts that she usually taught experientially through consultations and interactive presentations of the tools she created, I indulged my passion for general systems theory, integrative psychology, Buddhism, and learning and creativity. You'll find metaphors and insights drawn from these areas throughout the book. Together, Lon and I refined our laypersons' understanding of quantum physics and the rich examples and analogies it offers to express Lon's insights into the magic of interdependence, co-creation, and self-transformation.

It was very exciting to make new use of my years of teaching about dynamic complementarity and general systems theory and to discover new ways of presenting and applying those models as we worked out the language to convey Lon's intuitive perception of the significance of the changes we're observing in our lives. We adapted the concepts of interdependence, interconnectedness, and self-transcendence at the core of general systems theory to present her approach to co-creation, self-transformation, and contribution in the multidimensional reality she sees emerging from the apparent chaos of our time. Her vision of the potential for creativity that arises from chaos reframes what many around us see as signs of catastrophe—she sees signs of transformation to a reality that is more complex, inclusive, and abundant than the one we've been conditioned to perceive.

Working on this book with Lon has been a catalyst for growth and transformation for me. If you take it up with a desire to use its ideas and practices to guide you on a journey of self-exploration and self-transformation, this book might do for you what it did for me. Like any pilgrim traveling into new territory, with an eye for mystery and an ear attuned to an inner voice, you will find yourself inhabiting a world enriched with greater possibility than you ever imagined when you set out, and you'll have a much better measure of your unlimited potential to collaborate in the realization of that world of possibility.

—Diane Young, PhD

Diane Young, PhD, has taught writing as self-evolution by engaging people in creative thinking, learning, and growth in many settings. She consults in course curriculum development, collaborates with writers editing fiction and nonfiction, illustrates her own poetry and fiction, and is writing a book on cultivating creativity.

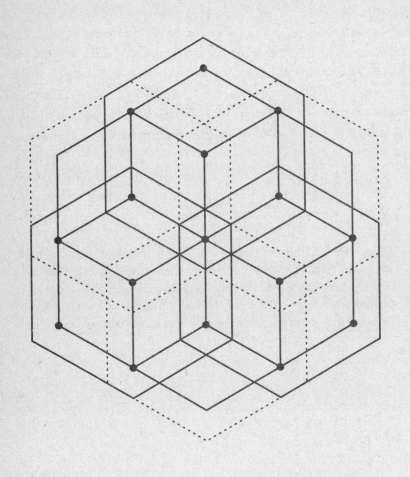

# ACKNOWLEDGMENTS

For Kai, whose fearless commitment to truth and love gave me courage to bring my magic out.

For Diane, whose guidance gave structure and foundation to the journey.

For Erika, whose unwavering support made me feel strong and unconditionally loved.

For Michele, who asked me to write this book for her so the not-so-obvious could be seen and understood.

For all the other beautiful souls that touched my heart and who sparked my magic with theirs.

And last but not least, for a world that is worthy of our belief in magic.

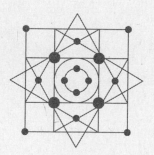

# RESOURCES

## Lon Art: Modern-Day Mandalas

I use sacred geometry to create "modern-day mandalas" to inspire original thought and activate thinking beyond the everyday so you can make real changes in your life. All my pieces address large concepts that are the core of the human experience: concepts like magic, love, healing, abundance, connection, intimacy, and multi-dimensionality, for instance. These concepts are fundamental to the way we create our world, our lives, and our relationships with each other. By diving deep into their essence, we can explore our relationships with the qualities they represent and how they are showing up in our lives.

To create "abundance," for instance, we have to understand what the concept means to us, what it takes for us to *feel* abundant, and what stands in the way of always experiencing that. This applies to many concepts that we loosely refer to as being desirable. Often, on further exploration, we discover that our beliefs are in the way of actually realizing these concepts. We all want love, for instance . . . yet many of us are walking around feeling unworthy of it. This feeling is often generated by programs that are deeply buried in the subconscious. These hidden beliefs block us from performing our magic and creating the outcomes in our lives that we really want, until we bring them into our awareness and release or transform them.

## Soul Portraits

In chapter 7 we talked about how most of us want to experience a sense of a higher purpose in our lives, the feeling that we contribute to the whole. We are growing and evolving our awareness in ways that enable us to express that higher purpose. Many of us have a feeling that we are destined to become something larger than we are now, that we were born to do something specific. We dream of our futures and the things we want to create; we set goals; we push ourselves to do better, be better, make a difference, leave a footprint. Our fulfillment often comes from the feeling that we are living our vision, our "soul purpose."

## A Soul Portrait is a mirror of your soul.

We already saw that everyone has their own very specific energy or vibration. And just like a radio receiver can tune in to the frequency of specific radio stations, we can tune in to the frequency of you. The you that is beyond your physical body. The you that is multidimensional, vibrational, and deeply connected, entangled, and in co-creation with something much larger. The you that is your soul. We can then translate the multidimensional you into a sacred geometry image that activates your connection to your soul and your purpose here on earth. You will know you've glimpsed your soulself when your subconscious and your soul recognize you in this vision.

Since I express myself through form and color and use sacred geometry as a way of seeing the world, it has become a visual language for me. Having developed skills as a graphic artist, I can translate my Perceptual Mode vision into an expression in the 3D world. I use sacred geometric principles, shapes and forms, colors, numerology, and symbology to create a representation of a person in a language that is universal and beyond words. The subconscious and the soul will intrinsically understand this language, as it is at the core of our very essence. I call these creations Soul Portraits because each is a multidimensional reflection of a soul and its purpose.

I include an in-depth explanation of each Soul Portrait's meaning, a description of the imagery, and a reading of how it all applies to the subject's personal soul journey so that the power of the portrait, which is a unique (multidimensional) activation, gets expanded and amplified by words that resonate with the linear mind as well. The portrait is a constant reminder of who the person really is, at their core, on a soul level, and what they are here to do. The explanation opens up ways of seeing further into the portrait the longer the person lives with it. The portrait will help the person become the best possible version of themself as they continue evolving.

My own Soul Portrait is on the front cover of this book. It is called *Illumination*, reflecting my "soul purpose" of bringing the unknown into the light so it can be seen and understood.

For more information about personal Soul Portraits, please visit my website at https://lon-art.com.

# READERS CLUB GUIDE QUESTIONS

This readers club guide for *Modern Merlin* includes discussion questions from the author. The suggested questions are intended to help your reading group find new and interesting angles and topics for your discussion. We hope that these ideas will enrich your conversation and increase your enjoyment of the book.

1. What experience while you were reading the book gave you your first sense of multidimensionality?

2. Given your experience of multidimensionality, what has the title come to mean to you? Did you research the story of Merlin and Camelot to expand your understanding of the title? How much did you know about that myth before reading this book?

3. How did reading the book expand your perception of reality?

   a) Did it engage you in the questions being raised by quantum physicists?

   b) Did it inspire you to research sacred geometry?

   c) If you came to the book with any understanding of Buddhism, Islam, Judaism, Hinduism, or Christianity, did it inspire you to research those belief systems and their contemplative practices to deepen your relationship with them?

4. Did you do the suggested tune-ins at the end of every chapter? Did you find them valuable? Give an example of how a particular tune-in shifted your perspective or expanded your experience.

5. Did you find that the book gave you good guidance on how to shift into Perceptual Mode?

   a) How has being able to access Perceptual Mode affected your understanding of yourself?

   b) How has being able to access Perceptual Mode affected your understanding of reality?

   c) Has your attitude toward yourself changed as a result of your experience of Perceptual Mode? How about your feelings toward others?

   d) How has your experience in Perceptual Mode changed your understanding of what it means to be in relationship to others?

   e) How has the book, particularly as it has invited you to enter Perceptual Mode and multidimensionality, changed your understanding of the world and your role in it?

6. Are there other modes of perception that you think you bring to your experience that you didn't use before reading this book?

7. How has using the practices and exercises offered in this book affected your understanding of health and well-being? Of success? Of happiness? Of prosperity? Of contribution? Of love?

8. How do you use the Modern Merlin Transformation Tool? What transformations do you notice in yourself and in your relationship to the world since you've begun using it?

9. If you were to teach someone you care about one of the practices or exercises you learned in this book, which one would you share? Why that one?

10. Have you found that your experience of yourself as a creative person—having the ability to create—has changed while reading this book? Have you discovered new forms of creativity? Or maybe returned to ones you haven't practiced for a while? Or even strengthened the creative practice you brought with you to the book?

11. What other books would you recommend as readings that would build on or complement *Modern Merlin*?

12. If you could talk to the author, what burning question would you want to ask?

13. If you could talk with any of the writers quoted in the text, who would it be and why? What would you ask?

14. Are you familiar with the author's sacred geometry work? Are you intrigued to check it out?

15. Would you want to do the Modern Merlin online course after reading the book?

# MODERN MERLIN
# TRANSFORMATION TOOL

These templates will support you in uncovering the beliefs that are at the core of your thoughts and feelings, give rise to the stories you tell yourself and others, and therefore ultimately make up the vibrational signal you send out into the Universe and the quantum field. Remember, for you to be a powerful Modern Merlin who is in full co-creation with the Universe, your signal needs to be in full alignment with your wish or vision. You therefore must look at the beliefs that are at the core of your way of being.

## The Power of Beliefs

As you've learned, your beliefs are at the core of your magical power: the beliefs you have about the world, the beliefs you have about other people, and most of all the beliefs you have about yourself. Those beliefs can affect your ability to express your potential and to create a life you find joy in.

What follows are some guidelines for revealing your personal beliefs by reflecting on the stories you tell yourself and those you tell others. Because our beliefs often carry hidden assumptions, you'll also find guidelines for unearthing those assumptions so that you can challenge and transform them (if they're limiting) or consciously embrace and strengthen them (if they're supportive of your goals).

## Explore, Transform, and Rewrite

The Transformation Tool will guide you in these practices:

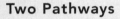

- ▲ **exploring** your beliefs and the assumptions embedded in them

- ▲ **transforming or strengthening** those beliefs into evolved beliefs by challenging or refining the assumptions embedded in them

- ▲ **rewriting the stories** or discovering the activities that can help you align with those evolved beliefs

## Two Pathways

The Transformation Tool provides two pathways to guide you to a goal: one that follows the path of *concepts* and one that follows the path of *stories*. Both are equally powerful in guiding you to new insights and discoveries about the beliefs that are hidden in your subconscious. You can work with either approach, or you might find that you can work with both. You can choose a goal to help you discover concepts that are at the core of your beliefs, or you can explore how the stories you tell shape those beliefs.

This dual process can be seen as an emerging double helix: one spiral of evolution or transformation springing out of your work with a concept, the other springing out of your work with a story. The connections between these two paths will help you see ways of taking what you learn in Perceptual Mode and using it to manifest what you want in your life. You may find that it's helpful to record your explorations and whatever grows out of them in a journal.

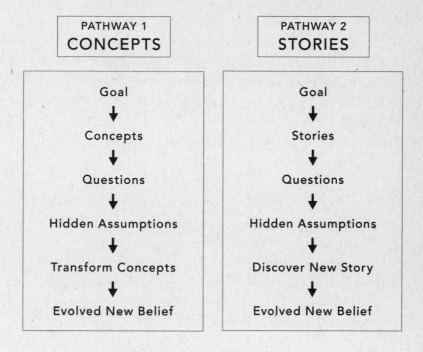

## Pathway 1: Concepts

**1.** Choose a goal

**2.** Explore the concept(s)

**3.** Transform the beliefs

## 1. Choose a Goal

Goals can help us focus our investigation into our beliefs, so the first set of prompts begins with identifying a goal. Your goals may reflect your wish to make a change in one or more areas of your life; for example, your goal could be that you would like to be in a romantic relationship. Most of the goals we set for ourselves are layered, and by taking a closer look at them we can discover the desires that are truly at their cores. For instance, in our example of your desire to have a romantic relationship, we have to look at your relationship with the concept of love in general to understand your dynamic with romance in particular.

Keeping in mind the goal of a romantic relationship, contemplate the following:

▲ How do you want to **feel**? Maybe you would like to experience the feelings you associate with seeing yourself as a lovable person (joyful, attractive, interesting, approachable, open), or maybe you just want to feel loved (heard, seen, understood). As a general principle, sitting with any emotion in Perceptual Mode will open or heighten your sense of connection with Source.

▲ What is a **quality of energy** you'd like to experience or express? You want to *be loving* as an expression of the quality; you want to *be loved* as an experience. This could mean that you'd like to experience or express the energy of love; you want to be capable of love, compassion, sharing, commitment, and being present. This energy is giving, balanced, rooted deeply in self-worth and feeling part of a Creative Source that is abundant, always supportive, and loving.

▲ What is a **material or physical reality** you'd like to create? This could mean that you want to have a loving romantic partner in your life.

▲ What is a **relationship** you'd like to have or improve? This could mean that you want to create a new kind of romantic relationship, marriage, business partnership, or parenting style.

▲ What is a **contribution** you'd like to make? Do you want to be part of a co-creational relationship with a partner who has a vision of a romantic relationship that is aligned with yours? Your vision could be that you both support each other to realize your individual dreams while evolving the connection between you.

## 2. Explore the Concept(s)

Using Perceptual Mode, go inward to discover the concept you'd like to explore. Get comfortable; close your eyes if that feels good to you. Sit with your goal in mind and observe what arises. When a concept or image arises that resonates with you, stay with it and observe how it morphs and evolves as you hold it in relationship with your goal.

Let's say that the concept "love" came up when you were sitting with your goal of a romantic relationship, meaning you were thinking about romantic love and how and where it shows up in your life. Maybe you realized that you were actually looking at where love in general shows up in your life. Then when you contemplated love, the concept "rare" came up and you realized that it is actually a rare occasion when love shows up. Now, take that concept of "rare" and explore that.

### Questions to Contemplate

Consider what you've learned (while you were in Perceptual Mode) about the relationship between your goal and this concept and what it might tell you about your beliefs—in this case, your beliefs about love. Here are some questions you could ask yourself to achieve deeper insights:

▲ Do you consider yourself a lovable person?

▲ Are there certain qualities you have that make you lovable and attractive? Perhaps you are a great listener, or you are compassionate, understanding, and loyal?

▲ Did you consider love as something scarce, meaning you don't have enough of it in your life?

▲ Do you consider love to be rare? Does "scarce" feel different than "rare"?

▲ How does your feeling around love (your goal) shift when you connect it to the concept of "rare"?

▲ Can you consider "rare" as preciousness? Or richness? Perhaps you have plenty, or the perfect amount of it?

▲ Does that shift you to a sense of abundance?

▲ What makes you feel abundant?

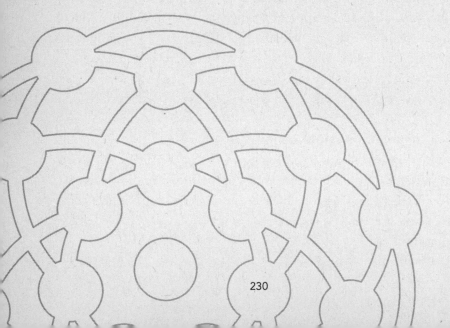

Once you find the pattern or relationship between your goal (love) and your concept (rare), stay with the image or sense of them. Allow them to interact and dance with each other and evolve your understanding of their dynamics. You might find that one concept leads to another, and that one to yet another. You might think about these emerging images or senses as a constellation of concepts. What insight into your goal emerges from them? Remember that multi-dimensionality is characterized by associative, non-linear thinking and imagining. Ideas that seem at first glance to be opposites in conflict can turn out to be complementary opposites dancing with each other.

### Record Your Discoveries

Perhaps you'd like to journal about your discoveries, since writing often helps us dive deeper into our own thought processes and uncover what is hidden in our subconscious. Or perhaps you like to do this through imagery—like drawing, painting, or doodling. You might even try sculpting with a medium you can shape with your hands, like clay, soft wire, or even papier-mâché. You might find that this is a good way for you to expand beyond your initial concept by exploring the constellation of concepts that arose in Perceptual Mode.

For example, in writing about how the concept "rare" shifted and morphed, you might feel that it would be interesting to look at "abundance" as a concept in relation to love. If so, go back into Perceptual Mode and invite "love" and "abundance" to dance with each other—perhaps you find that what emerges is a sense that love is limitless. You might find yourself creating a drawing that expresses a feeling of abundant love, or a clay form that captures a sense of preciousness and limitlessness at the same time. You can investigate as many concepts as you feel have resonance for you. Perhaps "inspiration" could be your next one on this journey.

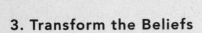

## 3. Transform the Beliefs

Now, reflect on what your Perceptual Mode exploration of "love" and its associated concepts has revealed to you about the beliefs you brought with you and how those beliefs could evolve to better support you in experiencing love.

▲ **What are the assumptions hidden in the concepts that emerged for you?**
Each transformation of the concepts reveals something about the assumptions that shaped the concepts.

For example, if "rare" began as "scarce," there may be an assumption like "not enough" behind that concept, and the concept of "rare" might have contributed to a belief like "I'm not worthy of something that's scarce, like being loved." If it morphed to "preciousness," there may be an assumption like "must be cared for or attended to" behind that concept, and that concept of "preciousness" might have contributed to a belief like "I'm not good at being in relationships, so I don't deserve what's precious; people who know how to take care of what's precious create a kind of richness or abundance for themselves, and I don't."

▲ **What deeper insights about your initial beliefs emerged when you contemplated your goal in relationship with the concepts?**
For example, when you first started contemplating your goal (love) you discovered that you began believing that love is scarce, that you're not worthy of something that's rare, that you aren't good at taking care of things so you don't deserve something as precious as love, and that you can't create the abundance that characterizes love.

232

Those are the beliefs you want to challenge and transform—and the evolution of the initial concept of "rare" to "precious" to "richness" to "abundance" gives you a kind of blueprint for that transformation. You're taking your evolved concepts and using them to construct an evolved belief about love.

For example, you could generate a new belief about yourself: you are rare (there's only one of you) and precious (you are unique). There is only one of you in the whole universe, and people want to experience your unique and authentic self. In your contemplation, you arrived at a sense of love being both precious and limitless. If you consider the concept "love is limitless," you may find that you experience a sense of your connection to Source. You came from a loving Source and you will always be loved by this Source. As Source is infinite, there is an abundance of love, always. For everyone.

How could you not resonate with love and express it, given that you have its qualities in yourself? How could someone else not resonate with you, as you embody all the qualities that make a loving relationship successful?

Sit with this transformed and transformational belief in Perceptual Mode. Allow it to grow, expand, and permeate you. If you're keeping a journal, this is a great time to expand your initial map and fill in the details of your journey.

You can add detail to this map as you write in (or draw) the features of the landscape you've travelled through: you can record the morphing of concepts, the way one led to another, the way you carried forward what you learned from one leg of the journey to the next, and how what you carried transformed you as you moved toward creativity. You could even sculpt a souvenir of each concept that expresses its evolution and new form, if you "think through your hands" that way, and then describe it in your journal. The point is to capture the basic journey from where you began to where you've arrived.

Whether or not you've recorded your travels through the concepts around love, you are now ready to experience being loving in any domain. As you return to the 3D world, carry this belief with you and sustain your awareness of it as much as you can. Be open to all the ways you are expressing and experiencing love in your life. When you feel that you're ready, put this new belief into practice by focusing on any specific expression of your goal.

## Pathway 1: Concepts Flow Sheet

On the next page you'll find an example of an initial flow sheet for this exercise based on the goal of wanting more love. It shows you how you might make a basic map of the journey you took as you explored your goal and the concepts associated with it.

The page after that is the same flow sheet, but now empty, so you can use it for your own flow of discoveries and transformation. If you would like to print this flow sheet so you can use it whenever you want to explore and transform any belief you encounter, you can download a template from my website at https://lon-art.com /modern-merlin-templates.

PATHWAY 1
# CONCEPTS

| GOAL | I want to have more love in my life. |
|---|---|
| 3D GOAL | I want to be in a romantic relationship. |
| PERCEPTUAL MODE EXPLORATION | I rarely experience love because people just don't get me. |
| | I rarely experience love because I am not that interesting. |
| | I rarely experience love because I am unlovable. |
| CONCEPTS | Love |
| | Scarce |
| | Rare |
| | Precious |
| | Abundant |
| | Limitless |
| QUESTIONS | Do you consider yourself an attractive person? |
| | Are there certain qualities that make you attractive and lovable? |
| | |
| | |
| | |
| HIDDEN ASSUMPTIONS | There is not enough love to go around. |
| | I am not worthy of something that scarce like being loved. |
| | I am not good at relationships. |
| | |
| | |
| TRANSFORM CONCEPTS | I don't deserve to have love. |
| | I am not good at relationships. |
| | Instead of love being rare, I am rare, unique even. |
| | Because I am unique, I am precious. |
| | I am rich in potential and desire. |
| | I am abundant in aspiration and energy. |
| CONSTRUCT EVOLVED BELIEF | I am unique and therefore precious. I have unique qualities to offer; I am therefore lovable. There is only one person like me in the whole universe. |
| | |

PATHWAY 1
# CONCEPTS

| GOAL | |
|---|---|
| **3D GOAL** | |
| PERCEPTUAL MODE EXPLORATION | |
| | |
| CONCEPTS | |
| | |
| | |
| | |
| | |
| | |
| QUESTIONS | |
| | |
| | |
| | |
| | |
| HIDDEN ASSUMPTIONS | |
| | |
| | |
| | |
| TRANSFORM CONCEPTS | |
| | |
| | |
| | |
| | |
| CONSTRUCT EVOLVED BELIEF | |
| | |
| | |

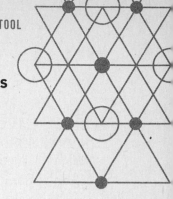

# Pathway 2: Stories

**1.** Choose a goal

**2.** Explore the story

**3.** Transform the beliefs

This basic template for reflection and Perceptual Mode practice works just as well if you use a story you tell about yourself (to others or to yourself) as it does if you use a concept. You can also work with a story others tell about you that you accept as "true" (for example, that story about something you did when you were three that you have no explicit memory of but that you have been taught tells you something about who you are).

## 1. Choose a Goal

Choose a goal you'd like to focus on achieving or progressing toward. Your goals may reflect your wish to make a change in one or more areas of your life. To contrast the two paths, let's stick with our example goal of wanting to be in a romantic relationship.

▲ How do you want to **feel**? Maybe you would like to have the feelings you associate with experiencing yourself as a lovable person (joyful, attractive, interesting, approachable, open), or maybe you just want to feel loved (heard, seen, understood). As a general principle, sitting with any emotion in Perceptual Mode will open or heighten your sense of connection with Source.

▲ What is a **quality of energy** you'd like to experience or express? You want to *be loving* as an expression of the quality; you want to *be loved* as an experience. This could mean that you'd like to experience or express the energy of love; you want to be capable of love, compassion, sharing, commitment, and being present. This energy is giving, balanced, rooted deeply in self-worth and feeling part of a Creative Source that is abundant, always supportive, and loving.

▲ What is a **material or physical reality** you'd like to create? This could mean that you want to have a loving romantic partner in your life.

▲ What is a **relationship** you'd like to have or improve? This could mean that you want to create a new kind of romantic relationship, marriage, business partnership, or parenting style.

▲ What is a **contribution** you'd like to make? You want to be part of a co-creational relationship with a partner who has a vision of a romantic relationship that is aligned with yours. Your vision could be that you both support each other to realize your individual dreams while evolving the connection between you.

## 2. Explore the Story

With your goal in mind, use Perceptual Mode to help you choose or discover the story you'd like to explore. Get comfortable; close your eyes if that feels good to you. Sit with your goal in mind and observe what arises. When a story arises that resonates with you, stay with it and observe how it morphs and evolves as you hold it in relationship with your goal. You'll find, as you did with concepts, that the first story will call up a second story—and that one might give rise to another. Notice what other stories emerge as you sit with your goal and this story in your awareness. Observe how they morph and evolve.

### Contemplate

Now consider what you have learned in Perceptual Mode about the relationship between your goal and these stories, and the connections among these stories. What does the relationship tell you about your beliefs (in this case, your beliefs about love)?

▲ Say the story that emerges initially is the one your mother told you about how she and your dad met at a time they were both very lonely and desperate and how they got together because they simply didn't have anybody else in their lives. They were struggling from the start in their relationship. Then your mom got pregnant with your sister, so they decided to get married. You were conceived after that because your mom did not want your sister to be an only child, like she had been. You were not conceived out of love.

Stay with your memory of this story and observe how it morphs and becomes richer in detail as it calls up other stories that resonate with it. Maybe you see how aware you were as a child of how many people were lonely inside their relationships, including your mom and dad . . . and how you yourself were lonely within the family.

You might feel that these stories capture exactly how it feels to be in relationships with others, how most of them are not based on being heard, seen, and understood. How the disconnect between your mom and your dad became your norm for what a romantic love relationship looks like. How you expected this to be true for your own relationships as well.

Going into Perceptual Mode has allowed you to find your way back to the source of the story: your experience of yourself (maybe even of your soulself!).

▲ Maybe the next story that floats up is one where you got involved in a romantic relationship in your early twenties. You knew deep down that there was no soul connection, but you thought your intellectual compatibility would be enough. You didn't believe that a "real" connection was possible anyway; you believed we are all ultimately on our own and that no one really sees and understands another. You were both unhappy in this relationship, and it eventually ended.

And that story calls up another one that resonates with those feelings of getting involved with people who are not a real match, of compromising yourself, of settling for less than what you really desire, and of feeling unworthy of "true love."

Observe what feelings, themes, or "lessons" emerge from these stories. See if there are any connections among them, especially if they show up more than once.

## 3. Transform the Beliefs

Now look at the feelings, themes, and lessons that emerged from these stories. What did your exploration reveal about the beliefs you have about love?

▲ **How have these feelings, themes, and lessons shaped your beliefs about love?**
Maybe these stories shaped a belief that love is hard work, that it means compromising yourself to a point where you cannot be your authentic self, that love means feeling lonely even when you're in a relationship. Perhaps you believe (romantic) love is just not for you.

▲ **What assumptions are hidden in this belief?**
That love is scarce, that love is not for you, that love is disappointing, unattainable, and pretty much impossible.
Now that you can see those hidden assumptions, challenge them by asking yourself if you believe them to be true for other people as well. Note what you believe to be true about love for other people.

▲ **What deeper insights about your initial beliefs emerged when you contemplated your goal in relationship to the stories you told?**
You can reflect on the feelings you've had when you've read stories, watched movies, or observed people who were happy in their relationships. You can look for moments when you felt loved and acknowledged, not just by a

romantic partner but by any other person, by a pet, or even just by life and the Universe itself (Source or God or Spirit). Imagine what you would feel like if you felt loved. If you felt seen, heard, and understood. Find some experiences when this happened to you. An example could be when you went to see a chiropractor for your back pain, and he made you feel completely seen and understood.

What do those feelings tell you about what love feels like to you? What lessons can you take away from them about what love means for you?

Transform your old beliefs about love by aligning them with or enlarging them to accommodate what you've learned about how you felt when you felt loved. When you felt that you belonged. You may give rise to a new belief about love that tells you it's fun, easy, and fulfilling, that there is more than enough love for everyone, as we are always supported, known, and loved by a higher power. You may believe that feeling seen, understood, and loved is possible for you in this lifetime. You will see that truth when you're resonating those energies, which are set in vibration when you remember love—the experience of love in any form (not just romantic love). You will resonate those energies whenever you remember the lived experience—the real story—that has been hidden *behind* the story you learned to tell over and over so that you could be safe, or meet others' expectations, or do the "right" thing . . .

Sit in Perceptual Mode with this transformed and transformational belief. Allow it to grow, expand, and permeate you. You are now ready to experience love in any domain.

As you return to the 3D world, carry this belief with you and sustain your awareness of it as much as you can in your everyday experience. Be open to all the ways you are expressing and experiencing love in your life. Your experiences with and observations of love—of feeling heard, seen, and understood in the present—will enable you to challenge and transform the lessons of the stories you have carried with you thus far. Be aware of the stories you tell yourself about love, and align them with your new beliefs. Allow these new stories to continue to expand your sense of love and strengthen your awareness of it. When you feel you're ready, put this new belief into practice by focusing on any specific expression of your goal.

## Pathway 2: Stories Flow Sheet

On the next page you'll find an example of an initial flow sheet for this exercise based on the goal of wanting more love. It shows you how you might make a basic map of the journey you took as you explored your goal and the stories associated with it.

The page after that is the same flow sheet, but now empty, so you can use it for your own flow of discoveries and transformation.

If you would like to print this flow sheet so you can use it whenever you want to explore and transform any belief you encounter, you can download a template from my website at https://lon-art.com/modern-merlin-templates.

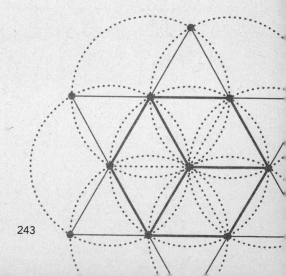

PATHWAY 2
# STORIES

| GOAL | I want to have more love in my life. |
|---|---|
| 3D GOAL | I want to be in a romantic relationship. |
| PERCEPTUAL MODE EXPLORATION | Parents' marriage |
| | My marriage in my twenties |
| | Other relationships in which I settled |
| | |
| | |
| | |
| | |
| | |
| | |
| LESSONS OF THE STORIES | Settling out of loneliness |
| | Settling out of inability to believe that I can be myself in a marriage |
| | Settling out of inability to believe that I can find a soul mate |
| | |
| | |
| HIDDEN ASSUMPTIONS | If I don't accept this partner, I will never have one. |
| | If I am fully myself, I won't be loved. |
| | I am not capable of attracting a soul mate. |
| | |
| CHALLENGE OLD STORIES AND THEIR LESSONS | I can be without a partner and still experience love. |
| | I don't need a partner to feel loved. |
| | The more fully I am myself, the easier I will draw love to me. |
| | Being fully myself is the strongest vibration to attract a soul mate. |
| | |
| | |
| CONSTRUCT EVOLVED BELIEF | By being fully myself I will experience love. |
| | |
| | |

## PATHWAY 2
# STORIES

| GOAL | |
|---|---|
| **3D GOAL** | |
| **PERCEPTUAL MODE EXPLORATION** | |
| | |
| | |
| | |
| | |
| | |
| | |
| | |
| **LESSONS OF THE STORIES** | |
| | |
| | |
| | |
| **HIDDEN ASSUMPTIONS** | |
| | |
| | |
| | |
| **CHALLENGE OLD STORIES AND THEIR LESSONS** | |
| | |
| | |
| | |
| **CONSTRUCT EVOLVED BELIEF** | |
| | |
| | |

# ABOUT THE AUTHOR

Lon is an internationally acclaimed sacred geometry artist, author, and creator of two bestselling and award-winning oracle decks, the *Sacred Geometry Activations Oracle* and the *Sacred Geometry of Relationships Oracle*. As founder of Lon Art, she offers tools for transformation, readings, and personal Soul Portraits that connect you to your soul purpose. Lon's work inspires original thought and activates thinking beyond the everyday, so you can make real changes in your life and become the best possible version of yourself. For more information, please visit https://lon-art.com.